MW00426347

The
SCHOOL LEADER'S
Guide to
Restorative School Discipline

The
SCHOOL LEADER'S
Guide to
Restorative School Discipline

Luanna H. Meyer
Ian M. Evans

CORWIN
A SAGE Company

CORWIN
A SAGE Company

FOR INFORMATION:

Corwin
A SAGE Company
2455 Teller Road
Thousand Oaks, California 91320
(800) 233-9936
www.corwin.com

SAGE Publications Ltd.
1 Oliver's Yard
55 City Road
London EC1Y 1SP
United Kingdom

SAGE Publications India Pvt. Ltd.
B 1/I 1 Mohan Cooperative Industrial Area
Mathura Road, New Delhi 110 044
India

SAGE Publications Asia-Pacific Pte. Ltd.
3 Church Street
#10-04 Samsung Hub
Singapore 049483

Copyright © 2012 by Corwin

All rights reserved. When forms and sample documents are included, their use is authorized only by educators, local school sites, and/or noncommercial or nonprofit entities that have purchased the book. Except for that usage, no part of this book may be reproduced or utilized in any form or by any means, electronic or mechanical, including photocopying, recording, or by any information storage and retrieval system, without permission in writing from the publisher.

Printed in the United States of America

Library of Congress Cataloging-in-Publication Data

Meyer, Luanna H.

The school leader's guide to restorative school discipline / Luanna H. Meyer and Ian M. Evans.

p. cm.
Includes bibliographical references and index.

ISBN 978-1-4129-9860-4 (pbk.)

1. School discipline—United States—Handbooks, manuals, etc. 2. Behavior modification—United States—Handbooks, manuals, etc. 3. School management and organization—United States—Handbooks, manuals, etc. 4. School administrators—United States—Handbooks, manuals, etc. I. Evans, Ian M., 1944- II. Title.

LB3012.2.M49 2012
371.5—dc23   2012001934

This book is printed on acid-free paper.

Certified Chain of Custody
SUSTAINABLE FORESTRY INITIATIVE
Promoting Sustainable Forestry
www.sfiprogram.org
SFI-01268
SFI label applies to text stock

Acquisitions Editor: Jessica Allan
Associate Editor: Allison Scott
Editorial Assistant: Lisa Whitney
Production Editor: Amy Schroller
Copy Editor: Lana Arndt
Typesetter: C&M Digitals (P) Ltd.
Proofreader: Sally M. Scott
Indexer: Sylvia Coates
Cover Designer: Lisa Riley
Graphic Designer: Karine Hovsepian
Permissions Editor: Karen Ehrmann

12 13 14 15 16 10 9 8 7 6 5 4 3 2 1

Contents

List of Tables and Figures

Tables

Figures

Acknowledgments

Corwin gratefully acknowledges the contributions of the following reviewers:

Carol S. Cash
Assistant Clinical Professor
Virginia Tech
School of Education
Richmond, VA

Lyman Goding
Principal (Retired)
Plymouth Community
    Intermediate School
Sandwich, MA

Steve Knobl
High School Principal
Pasco County Schools
Gulf High School
New Port Richey, FL

Neil MacNeill
Principal
Ellenbrook Primary School
Ellenbrook, WA
Australia

Natalie Marston
Principal
Anne Arundel County Public
    Schools
Central Special Education Center
Edgewater, MD

Jadi K. Miller
Principal
Elliott Elementary School
Lincoln, NE

Mary Reeve
Director, Special Education and
    Gifted Services
Gallup McKinley County
    Schools
Gallup, NM

About the Authors

Luanna H. Meyer is professor of education (research) and director of the Jessie Hetherington Center for Educational Research at Victoria University in New Zealand. She is also professor emerita at Syracuse University in the United States and adjunct professor at Griffith University in Australia. Since receiving her PhD from Indiana University, she held faculty positions at the University of Hawai'i, the University of Minnesota, Syracuse University, and Massey University prior to her current position. While at Syracuse University, she cofounded the Inclusive Elementary and Special Education Teacher Education Program and coordinated the doctoral program in special education. She also led numerous federally funded research and development projects, including a 5-year research institute on the social relationships of children and youth with diverse abilities and the 10-year New York Partnership for Statewide Systems Change.

Throughout her career as a teacher educator and educational researcher, Luanna has been committed to developing practical, evidence-based approaches that can be implemented in real-life, typical situations and settings. She works closely with school leaders, teachers, and behavior specialists toward achieving inclusive schools where all children and youth belong and feel valued. Her contributions to the development of positive approaches to behavior problems are acknowledged by her appointment to the Technical Review Committee on Behavior for the National Center for Students with Disabilities who Require Intensive Interventions led by the American Institutes for Research. She was among the first to demonstrate that even the most severe behavior can be managed with positive approaches, supported by her published research conducted in typical settings with children with severe behavior disorders, autism, and other disabilities. In New Zealand, her current federally funded projects include research on culturally responsive behavioral intervention in schools; culturally responsive pedagogies for teachers; effective school-based behavioral intervention practices; and the impact of assessment design on student motivation and achievement in secondary schools across the curriculum. A major focus of this work is on effective policy and practice to meet the needs of an increasingly diverse regular education school community.

Luanna has been invited to speak in eight countries and 30 U.S. states about her work, and she has published more than 120 journal articles and book chapters. Her 12 books include *Making Friends: The Influences of Culture and Development; Critical Issues in the Lives of People with Severe Disabilities; Behavioral Intervention: Principles, Models, and Practices; The Syracuse Community-Referenced Curriculum Guide; Nonaversive Intervention for Behavior Problems: A Manual for Home and Community;* and *An Educative Approach to Behavior Problems: A Practical Decision Model.* Just as important, Luanna is a proud parent and grandparent.

 **Ian M. Evans** is professor of psychology at Massey University in New Zealand. After receiving his PhD at the University of London's Institute of Psychiatry, he taught behavior assessment and therapy for many years at the University of Hawai'i while also serving as consultant psychologist to specialized programs for children and adults with very complex developmental needs. He founded the Hawai'i Association for Autistic Children and was appointed commissioner on the Governor's State Planning and Advisory Council for Developmental Disabilities. At this time, he and Luanna Meyer began their collaborative work in the public schools across the state, funded by a federal research grant on children's challenging behavior. They have published together on learning and behavior, including major meta-analyses on effective interventions and the earliest practical books on behavior problems for use by teachers and practitioners titled *Nonaversive Intervention for Behavior Problems* and *An Educative Approach to Behavior Problems.*

After becoming director of clinical psychology training at SUNY-Binghamton, Ian continued his focus on disabilities as well as leading the Binghamton Liberty Partnership Project. This intervention research was funded by state and federal grants to work with elementary schools in preventing school dropout, using a home-visitor model to enhance teacher-parent communication. His book *Staying in School: Partnerships for Educational Change* reports this work and that of colleagues across New York State evaluating initiatives in regular education to support children, families, and the schools. Since moving to New Zealand in 1995, he has been professor, clinical program director, and department head at the

University of Waikato and then Massey University. He also served as president of the New Zealand Psychological Society. His most recent work is teacher-focused to enhance the emotional atmosphere in elementary school classrooms, which has led to publication of a manual and a series of research reports. His lifelong commitment to children with autism and their families has been recognized by honors including life member of the advocacy group Parent-to-Parent and chairing the government's Living Guidelines Group of the *New Zealand Autism Spectrum Disorder Guideline*.

Ian has published six books, 54 book chapters, and over 100 refereed journal articles, and he serves on the editorial boards of five international journals. He is a fellow of the American Psychological Association and a fellow of the Royal Society of New Zealand. His other interests include photography, antiques of the Arts and Crafts period, taking long non-strenuous walks, wine tasting, and watching his grandchildren develop.

Introduction to the Guide

This guide for principals and other school leaders is one of three guides comprising a comprehensive approach to restorative school discipline for elementary, middle, and high schools. Each guide is

- *Evidence based*—drawing on the latest research in education and psychology on effective strategies for educative discipline in classrooms and schools
- *Inclusive*—schoolwide strategies that accommodate different behavior-support needs to ensure emotionally safe and secure learning environments that do not exclude children and youth
- *Restorative*—incorporating approaches that focus on making things right, not on retribution for things that have gone wrong
- *Practical*—disciplinary frameworks and intervention approaches that are doable in typical middle, junior high, and high schools with the kinds of resources and personnel generally available
- *Contextual*—socially valid principles and practices that fit comfortably in regular schools and typical classrooms and that reflect community values about how children and youth should be treated
- *Culturally responsive*—educationally meaningful guidelines for culturally responsive policy and practice in linguistically and culturally diverse school communities
- *User friendly*—presented in a succinct format respectful of the multiple responsibilities, busy schedules, and existing capabilities of educational personnel, incorporating theoretical constructs, references, and intervention descriptions directly relevant to each person's role in educative discipline. These recommendations are designed to fit within the realities of your individual school and school population.

PRACTICE OUTCOMES

This guide includes the information needed to develop the following outcomes for practice by principals and other school leaders:

1. *Establish a restorative discipline school community*—ensuring that the underlying values and driving forces of your school community are positive relationships, where every member of that community feels a sense of belonging, is valued, and accepts responsibility for the well-being of others.

2. *Agree on behavior expectations for the school community*—applied to children and adults in all school settings including classrooms, walkways, stairs, restrooms, cafeteria, assembly, library, gym/intramural sports facilities, school bus, and outdoor areas surrounding the school.

3. *Describe components of effective behavioral interventions*—understanding the framework for interventions to address challenging behavior in students in a positive way, based on current research relevant to schools.

4. *Support teams and networks*—facilitate planning by school personnel, families, and behavioral consultants working together to support students, with clear lines of communication and cooperation with other child and youth services such as mental health and social welfare services.

5. *Establish schoolwide restorative discipline policy*—fair, transparent, and ethical school rules and behavior consequences communicated across school personnel, families, and students. This includes threat assessment and a standard response protocol for school safety.

6. *Implement restorative practices and in-school suspension systems*—systems that provide ongoing support for a school policy of inclusion and that ensure that challenges and conflict are addressed without exclusion, retribution, and/or loss of mutual respect.

7. *Evaluate professional development issues for staff*—assessing for all personnel the skills and understandings needed to promote restorative discipline, culturally responsive practices, socioemotional support, and high expectations for learning and behavior.

8. *Sustainability and continuous improvement*—ongoing review and renewal processes to update evidence-based approaches and ensure that policy and practices align with current knowledge about effective schools.

Section I

Setting the Context

1 Restorative School Discipline

This chapter presents an overall picture of the features that provide the foundation for a restorative discipline approach to school policies and practices. It also offers a process for planning and introducing restorative discipline in the school, along with providing essential information for sharing with the school community toward ensuring ownership of a whole-school approach.

RESTORATIVE SCHOOL DISCIPLINE

This guide builds on a school ethos that we describe as "restorative school discipline." Restorative school discipline is not an add-on program for the purposes of behavior management, nor does it provide just another tool in the toolbox for staff to use to deal with student behavior. In contrast, restorative school discipline represents a school culture that permeates all aspects of school organization and relationships within the school as well as relationships between the school and its community. Fundamentally, restorative school practices recognize that schools are educational institutions, so policy and practice should be educative for individual children and the school community. Because schools are educational institutions, the school's response to children's behavior should be consistent with education's goals of supporting teaching and learning—not punishment, retribution, and exclusion. From the individual child's perspective, the school is acknowledged as a social community where every child belongs and where children's behavioral challenges are addressed through supportive, educational interventions. From a whole-school perspective, restorative practices have the development of positive relationships and peaceful resolution of conflict for staff and students as their primary aims.

Restorative school discipline is reflected in school and classroom practice at every level. Restorative school discipline concurs with the societal goal that the primary purpose of schools is to *educate.* This responsibility to educate goes beyond basic skills such as literacy, numeracy, and subject knowledge: it includes education for citizenship and becoming a contributing member of one's community. Grounded in certain key principles, restorative school discipline is educational in providing all members of the school community with the skills and understandings for positive social interactions, relationships that support learning, and peaceful resolution of problems and conflict.

Foundations of Restorative Practices

Restorative practices have their origins in the concept of restorative justice in the criminal justice system. From a restorative justice perspective, offenses are viewed as interpersonal conflict between victim and offender that need to be addressed by focusing on the source of the problem—within the relationship or interaction between victim and offender (Zehr, 1990, 2002). Historically, most criminal justice systems have emphasized retribution and punishment as the consequences of transgressions by offenders against victims of crime. Restorative justice approaches shifted away from *punishment and retribution,* particularly for young offenders and for less serious offenses, and toward creating the conditions that allowed for making things right—*restoration.* Nevertheless, restorative justice as used within the criminal justice system does not necessarily mean there will not be consequences for criminal offenses. Offenders may still be incarcerated or required to pay a fine for offenses, but there would be procedures sitting alongside those legal consequences designed to allow for the repair of conflict and healing of relationships. These might include, for example, a formal apology from the offender and payment of reparations to the victim.

The adaptation of restorative justice principles for use in schools by educators and families are commonly referred to as restorative practices, incorporating several key principles of restorative justice:

- *Interpersonal relationships*: Affirming positive interpersonal relationships in the school community without exclusion and deficit theorizing that places blame on individual children, families, or other persons
- *Personal dignity*: Preserving the personal dignity of all members of the school community, encompassing the idea that every person belongs, is valued and cared for, and has the right to be treated fairly

- *Mutual respect and understanding*: Sharing each person's perspective about what happened in conflict, accompanied by respect for different views as constructed realities with strong personal meaning for each participant
- *Restorative conferencing*: Commitment to conflict resolution and restoration of positive interpersonal relationships through conversation in a safe environment
- *Restitution*: Agreement regarding what needs to happen to set things right, defuse conflict, and restore positive relationships

Restorative school discipline as described in this guide is not a behavior management system. Yet it includes the key elements of positive behavior management described in general terms as "educative" (Evans & Meyer, 1985) and "nonaversive" (Meyer & Evans, 1989) as well as in specific models such as "positive behavior support" (Dunlap, Sailor, Horner, & Sugai, 2009; Sugai et al., 2005) and "positive behavior for learning" (Savage, Lewis, & Colless, 2011). While restorative school discipline utilizes strategies that were developed and validated through decades of behavior management intervention research, it differs from behavior management approaches in starting from relationship and interactions perspectives where the focus is on the whole-school organization and culture. This means that it is not a bottom-up approach that emphasizes descriptions of acceptable and unacceptable behavior within deficit intervention frameworks. Nor is it top-down in asserting school rules set by the administration whereby violations are viewed as transgressions against rules. Instead, restorative school discipline is people focused, accepting that positive and supportive relationships are crucial for learning to occur in educational environments so that conflict must be addressed by making amends where relationships will otherwise be damaged and even broken.

Children's developmental capacities are also relevant. For restorative practices to work, parents and teachers need to build on reasonable expectations of children at different ages to develop the skills and understandings underpinning restorative practices across the grades. Cavanagh (2007) provides helpful advice for schools about the developmental implementation of a restorative practices approach to conflict resolution. He describes how these approaches can build children's socioemotional capacities and help to prevent bullying. For this to happen, there needs to be an awareness of children's developmental abilities for restorative practices at different ages:

- *Ages 5–6*: Children can understand feelings by learning that everyone has feelings and that different people can have different feelings—that is, feelings may not be the same. Children start to develop empathy by bonding with one another in ways that allow them to see how the other child feels about something. This is the time when children begin to learn about what a friendship is, compared with simply playing with one another.

- *Ages 7–9*: Children now understand the dynamics of friendships and belonging to a group. They learn about listening, trusting, speaking honestly "from the heart," and they learn to be respectful of others. This is the age when children should begin to learn negotiation and mediation skills, rather than simply pushing one's own perspectives or desires at the expense of others.
- *Ages 10–11*: In addition to all the above skills and understandings, children can speak truthfully while showing respect—they can be diplomatic. They should develop peacemaking skills and know how to solve problems in groups (e.g., through conferencing).
- *Ages 12–14*: Younger teenagers can engage in restorative conversations that do not confuse the problem with the person. They can take on major responsibility to conduct problem-solving group conferences, either formally in classrooms or informally with a peer group and with friends.
- *Ages 15–17*: Older teenagers can facilitate communication between bullies and victims, restore dignity to both parties, and negotiate removal of blame and punishment.

Clearly, some expectations for restorative understandings will not be age appropriate: for example, adults should not expect 6-year-olds to be diplomatic in discussions about someone else's feelings, but children at this age can be expected to listen to how the other person feels and be able to repeat what the other person said as evidence of having listened. Nor do skills that may be developmentally reasonable develop simply through maturation: Most teenagers will not be good at engaging in "restorative conversations that do not confuse the problem with the person"—indeed most adults have difficulty with this! Teenagers may be developmentally ready to learn how to do this, but their skills in doing so will be the product of previous social skill development as well as current expectations and supports.

Key Characteristics of Schools That Support Restorative Practices

What might a school with restorative discipline policies and practices look like? There is a rich literature on restorative school practices in different parts of the world, and there have been large-scale evaluations of the effectiveness across schools (Kane et al., 2007). McCluskey et al. (2008) describe some of the key characteristics of a school using restorative practices to address behavioral challenges:

- There is a positive school climate inclusive of all students, where students have a strong sense of belonging rather than being at risk for exclusion.
- Students experience positive learning relationships with adults and one another, feel safe, have high regard for their school community, and are given the opportunity to make things right when things go wrong.
- Culturally responsive pedagogies of relations underpin the school's approach to diverse student populations.
- Staff focus on students' strengths, reject deficit explanations for failure, and take agency for successful educational outcomes for children and youth.
- Families feel welcome in the school, participate in activities designed for parents, regularly receive information about how their young person is doing, and are involved in supporting their child's education as appropriate including collaborating actively to address problems.
- Average daily attendance is high, all absences must be excused for valid reasons, and there is timely, daily follow-up by teacher and school when students are absent or tardy.
- Students receive support and encouragement meeting their educational and socioemotional needs, including positive classroom relationships with peers, teachers with high expectations, and pedagogies that enable them to achieve to the best of their abilities.
- Reasonable and well-understood behavior expectations for children and youth are agreed upon, specified, and shared across the school community.
- A comprehensive system of schoolwide restorative discipline policies and practices with clear definitions of behavior and consequences is in place and communicated widely throughout the school and with families.
- Ongoing backup supports are in place—including threat assessment, crisis management, and in-school suspension to deal with severe behavior problems.
- Restorative practices and mutual respect are the foundations for interactions across members of the school community, not retribution and punishment.
- Professionals assume *agency* for student outcomes in accepting responsibility to add value to every student's achievements each

year without exception or excuses attributed to background characteristics or challenges such as socioeconomic, linguistic, or environmental circumstances.

    o Children come to school with various characteristics, and any of these may challenge educators and schools. However, children's characteristics or their home situation cannot be allowed to justify low expectations for their behavior and achievement at school, and a good educational program with positive opportunities for individual learning can make all the difference.

The Importance of School Climate

A positive school climate is an important condition for restorative school discipline that sits alongside and supports teaching and learning. Cohen, McCabe, Michelli, and Pickeral (2009) describe four major aspects of school life that influence and shape positive school climate:

- *Safety*: Safety encompasses physical aspects such as attitudes about violence, clearly communicated rules, people in the school feeling physically safe, and school staff knowing and adhering to agreed crisis plans. At the social and emotional level for staff and students, there is respect for individual differences, conflict resolution is taught, and the response to bullying (including cyberbullying) is explicit and fair.
- *Pedagogy*: There is a focus on the quality of instruction including discursive teaching and active learning; social, emotional, and ethical learning; professional development and professionalism for staff; and school leadership beyond the managerial to encompass curriculum and instruction.
- *Relationships*: Relationships throughout the school highlight respect for diversity, shared decision making, and valuing of student and staff learning communities. There is collaboration across school and community, including access to and support for student and family assistance programs. Staff morale reflects connectedness with the school and high job satisfaction supported by evidence that both staff and students feel good about their school.
- *Environment*: The school environment is clean and well maintained; adequate space is available for instructional and extracurricular activities; materials and resources are adequate; support services are available when needed; and the school has an inviting aesthetic quality.

Case example: Mrs. Lucia Larroa had recently arrived as the new principal for Mesa Intermediate. At one of her first senior management team meetings, her deputy principal, Mr. Mike Mooney, raised the problem of staff morale. Specifically, he said that lots of students were being referred to his office for seemingly minor offenses and that, as he walked around the school, he heard quite a few teachers raising their voices and sounding angry. "I think you need to call a teacher meeting and let them know that yelling at kids is just not what this school is about," he suggested to Mrs. Larroa. "OK, Mike," she answered, "that's an idea, but it sounds a bit top down for a newcomer like me to get away with. What I'd like to do first is to get a snapshot of how the teachers view the climate of this school. What is their perspective on the values of the school and whether we support them? Would you all help me by passing out a questionnaire to the staff, assuring them of total confidentiality? The one I have in mind is the Wisconsin School Climate Survey.[1] Actually, come to think of it, that is one the staff can do anonymously online, and it asks useful questions about their feelings, the administration, their attitudes toward learning and students. Once we get this information, then we can start to address anything they feel less happy about—and I think it will show we are serious about improving the school climate in a proactive way." The management team agreed. Lucia was very pleased to get the following note from one of her teacher a few days later: "Dear Lucia, one of the questions in your survey was 'my administrator treats me with respect.' A few days ago I'd have answered 'disagree' but I had to answer 'strongly agree' because I think asking our views on the questionnaire demonstrated your respect for our opinions in a practical way. Thank you."

---

[1] Available online at www.dpi.state.wi.us/sig/improvement/process.html

The context for *The School Leader's Guide* is closely related to holistic ideas underlying the importance of school climate. This guide is designed for restorative school discipline, thus the emphasis throughout is on *safety* and *relationships*, rather than on pedagogy and the school environment. Of course, principals and school leaders work alongside their school communities, teachers, and other personnel to ensure that healthy physical environments and effective pedagogical practices provide a foundation for teaching and learning activities. Restorative school discipline will be affected by the quality of these aspects. Even if pedagogy and the school environment are not the focus of this guide, school leaders recognize and act on the strengths and challenges associated with the school's physical characteristics and the quality of its teaching staff and teaching. There will be opportunities to identify areas of overlap between aspects of school climate that can be addressed proactively through restorative school discipline and things that cannot be improved immediately such as the physical condition of a building or the qualifications of staff. Nevertheless, throughout the guide, we address the importance of keeping an eye on both the school environment and pedagogy to identify longer term needs for improvements that will enhance safety and relationships through restorative school discipline.

PLANNING AND ESTABLISHING RESTORATIVE PRACTICES

If your school has attended to the kinds of school climate issues included above, you are in a position to establish restorative practices in your school. This section of the guide describes how school leaders can approach the issue of restorative school discipline so that it can become well understood and *owned* by the school community rather than being seen as yet another pet project coming from the administration.

The restorative practices approach described throughout this guide is compatible with the Response to Intervention (RTI) model for identifying and addressing students' learning and behavioral needs. The 2004 reauthorized Individuals with Disabilities Education Improvement Act (IDEIA) in the United States provides for the use of models such as RTI by school districts as the process for determining student eligibility for special education services. The RTI model was recommended by the President's Commission on Excellence in Special Education (2002) and subsequently has been widely adopted by the states as a method for addressing children's learning and behavioral needs before referrals to special education, in the United States (see www.rti4success.org). According to Gresham (2005), the RTI approach requires that schools implement and document the effects of research-based interventions to address the needs of children who are experiencing difficulty in regular education. Rather than waiting for children to fail before they can be referred to special education, referrals to special education according to the RTI model involve documentation that schools have implemented evidence-based practices for the student and that he or she has not responded to the kinds of interventions available in regular education. Rather than the traditional sequence of refer-test-place, individualized assessment is done first whenever a student is struggling and used to evaluate the effectiveness of different interventions in regular education for that child. Restorative practices as described in this book have a strong international research base for implementation in regular classrooms as well as—at a more intensive case conferencing level—with individual children who exhibit serious behavior problems.

Thus, the guide aligns with the RTI model in providing prevention and intervention supports at three increasing levels of intensity. At Level 1, referred to as primary prevention, schools must document that they have in place research-based programs in regular education shown to be effective for all children, including those who are culturally and linguistically diverse. At this level, students should experience academic curricula (e.g., reading programs) and classroom organizational structures (e.g., cooperative learning) for which effectiveness evidence exists. Documentation is required to support claims that a child is nonresponsive to educational services at this level in order to move to Level 2, referred to as secondary prevention. At this more intensive level, students would participate in research-based, specialized small-group or embedded intervention to address difficulties. If evidence reveals that a student does not respond to Level 2 interventions, Level 3 or tertiary prevention interventions would be implemented. Level 3 interventions are more specialized and individualized; they can include referral to special education services or, in some versions of the model in some U.S. states, special education may encompass an additional Level 4.

A critical feature of RTI is that referral for specialized services and interventions requires evidence that the student did not respond positively to good practice in the regular classroom (Level 1) and even small-group or other supplemental tutorial services (Level 2). Schools must be able to provide evidence that proactive strategies at less intensive levels have been tried and have not worked with learning and behavioral challenges before students can be referred to special education for more intensive services (Cheney, Flower, & Templeton, 2008; Fuchs, Fuchs, & Stecker, 2010).

Restorative Practices as Prevention and Intervention

Restorative school discipline provides a comprehensive framework and set of practices that have been empirically validated as effective at three levels:

- *Primary prevention*: Restorative school discipline is the foundation for a positive school climate that encourages and supports teaching and learning. It also provides the framework for developing social and emotional competencies for caring relationships and peaceful resolution of conflict for staff and students. In the RTI model, this level is referred to as Level 1 (Campbell & Anderson, 2008).
- *Secondary prevention*: Restorative school discipline encompasses systematic, positive, and evidence-based practices that have been

demonstrated to be effective in addressing challenging behaviors that occur despite positive schoolwide primary prevention. These practices include conferencing and mediation as well as formal processes for restoration of relationships to repair harm and prevent future incidents. Secondary prevention approaches are also designed to address the needs of children who typically require small group interventions and individualized support services on at least a temporary basis at different times in their school careers (generally considered to be approximately 15% of the school population). These services are fit within the overall culture of restorative school discipline, not as something added or different. This is Level 2 or secondary prevention in the RTI literature (see www .rti4success.org).

- *Tertiary prevention*: Within an overall framework of restorative school discipline, the model also encompasses individualized interventions and support services likely to be long term and ongoing for that small percentage of the school population (approximately 3% to 5%) who present significant and sometimes ongoing behavioral challenges in classrooms and schools. However, for these children as well, intervention is consistent with the principles and practices of the restorative approach. One feature that differentiates restorative discipline at this level is that, unlike retributive models or other approaches that use restorative practices only as another tool in the toolbox, even children who exhibit serious behavioral challenges are not excluded from the school community but are provided support to restore and repair while remaining in school and doing their work. This level of intervention is referred to as tertiary prevention in the literature and may involve special education referral and services (Walker et al., 1996).

Restorative School Discipline Planning

Once the school leader has made a commitment to undertake restorative school discipline, there are a number of steps needed to ensure that the approach is embedded within the school with full ownership from the school community—necessary if restorative school discipline is to work.

The following steps should be taken before putting the model into place or attempting to use isolated aspects of the approach described in this guide:

Step 1: At an upcoming scheduled meeting of your school leadership team, the principal should put the issue on the agenda and introduce a discussion paper about restorative school discipline for implementation consideration at your school, effective at the start of the next full school year. Restrict this paper to one to two pages (see the sample discussion paper provided at the end of this chapter) and have a small number of published references available for anyone who would like to read more about this work. Talk about the paper briefly but indicate it will be a full discussion item at the next meeting, with no decisions taken until after that time. Ask for one to two volunteers from the senior management team who will commit to reviewing the materials and addressing specific questions at the next meeting. Ask specifically for the senior school leader who generally deals with behavior issues to be part of this small group.

Step 2: At that next meeting (1 to 2 weeks later), place the item on the agenda for up to 30 minutes of discussion, led by the school principal and those who volunteered to also present information. Whether or not you proceed to Step 3 now depends on the level of interest in and/or resistance to restorative school discipline by your senior leadership team. Step 2 may actually require a series of meetings to ensure that your management team supports what needs to be a schoolwide commitment. Someone on your senior management team might have a traditional view of discipline referred to as "old school" with, for example, strong opinions that students should listen to and adhere to school rules—not help to make them and even question their fairness. Generally, you'll know about such differences in approach, and these will have to be addressed on a number of matters—not just the adoption of restorative school disciplinary practices.

Step 3: Once you have the commitment of your school leadership team, you are ready to approach your district superintendent. This should be primarily for communication purposes to inform the superintendent that your school intends to proceed, but the district office may also be able to connect you with relevant resources and expertise. It may even be that there are other schools in the district investigating and considering a fresh approach to challenges, so this information allows you to connect with potential support networks. The district leadership may also raise issues that your plans will need to take into account.

Step 4: You are now ready to approach your school board. Begin with a personal discussion with the chair of your board so that he or she understands what restorative school discipline would mean for the school. Schedule a brief presentation at an upcoming school board meeting in which you will signal that your school is starting a planning process that will be reflected in a new approach at your school with the start of the following school year. Provide a one-page handout for members of the board that is similar to the one provided to your senior leadership team and includes a reference to a website or other materials that interested board members can read. Make clear that you'll come back to the board with a fuller description of developments at a later meeting, providing plenty of time for discussion at the discretion of the board. Be prepared at this stage to answer questions about safety for students and staff.

Step 5: Next, introduce the plan to staff across the school. At secondary schools, you might begin this process by discussing the plans at the next scheduled meeting of heads of departments; soon after, introduce the plan at a general staff meeting. At elementary schools and at small schools at any level, you'll want to introduce the plan to the wider teaching staff right away. Recruit interest in serving on an in-house steering group that will be established and let everyone know you are happy to discuss the plan with staff individually if anyone would like to do so.

Step 6: Establish the in-house steering group that includes representatives from the school community. This group should include students, and you should decide for your school the best way to identify student members (at many schools, you might approach the student council and ask for one to two students to join the group). Your goal in establishing this steering group is to make ownership by the broader school community more visible and to provide direct support for the plan so that no one person is in the position of having to effect schoolwide change alone (including the principal). This in-house steering group should be chaired by the member of your leadership team who typically deals with behavior challenges at the school, and membership should be decided based on your school's typical practices for establishing such groups.

Step 7: The first actions of the in-house steering group will be to integrate with related school initiatives (such as developing social skills or a project designed to foster emotional literacy) and available resources to support the plan; review existing behavior management policies and practices; specify a new relationship management policy; and design a timetable in order to introduce restorative school discipline at the start of the next school year.

Step 8: Identify the evidence that your school will use to evaluate the effectiveness of the new approach, including objective outcome data such as exclusion figures; recorded bullying incidents; attendance; office discipline referrals (including different seriousness levels); and referrals for suspension/exclusion (which will be managed as in-school suspension as part of restorative practices; see Chapter 6 in this guide). Establish a system and person with overall responsibility to prepare a formal report on these data once each quarter during the school year, then summarized annually; a written report should be shared with constituents and your board but will also be presented orally to staff each quarter and to students at least once a year (e.g., at school assembly).

Step 9: Anticipate ongoing discussions to refine and revise your school's approach to restorative school discipline. Never shut down resistance but instead listen carefully to concerns and ask those who seem dubious to tell you what evidence they would need to persuade them that it is working well; then commit to collecting this evidence as part of the evaluation. Also, press for specific suggestions about how to improve the school's implementation of restorative practices. Finally, an excellent fallback position whenever someone remains unconvinced that the school is taking the right approach is to ask for cooperation and support for an implementation trial period. Remind staff that RTI practices already require documentation of the effects of interventions on students who exhibit challenging behaviors, so the school will have evidence of whether the new approach is making a difference. Promise staff that there will be evaluative data kept about whether the approach is working and if aspects need to be changed, and commit in advance to a formal review date involving your staff in discussions of results.

You know that school change can be a slow process. Your annual summary of evidence should tell you if your school is making progress, and ongoing meetings with the steering group and others will allow you to keep track of the extent to which there is ownership of restorative practices at your school. The annual summary will also tell you if major modifications for your approach are needed, and ongoing evidence should inform periodic refinements to the school's restorative practices. Most would argue that meaningful, whole-school cultural change requires more than a year or two, and you should allow 3 to 5 years for this important shift in supporting students and staff to become embedded.

SUMMARY

This chapter provides an overview of the essential features of schools committed to restorative practices. The chapter begins by emphasizing the overall importance of attending to school climate and then introduces

> ## Discussion Paper: What Is Restorative School Discipline?
>
> *Background*: Restorative practices in schools have been implemented internationally as guided by Zehr (1990) and many others. Restorative practices are based on a restorative justice view that offenses represent conflict between people that is best addressed by working to restore relationships and making things right, not by blaming and punishing that is focused on retribution.
>
> *Definition*: Restorative school discipline is a whole-school ethos or culture comprising principles and practices to support peacemaking and solve conflict through healing damaged relationships and making amends where harm has been done while preserving the dignity of everyone involved.
>
> *Key Features:*
>
> - Restorative, not retributive, culture of inclusion in the school
> - Curriculum focus on relationships among staff and students including support for enhancing skills and understandings for restorative conversations and conflict prevention and resolution
> - Restorative policies and practices reflecting a whole-school approach to positive relationships, behavioral challenges, and solving conflict through restorative practices
> - Processes for mediation, shuttle mediation, and peer mediation in classrooms and schoolwide
> - Processes for restorative meetings, informal conferences, classroom conferences, and formal conferences
> - School rules, guidelines, and systems that are transparent and fair in response to incidents and threats that require staff and students to be protected from harm or potential harm
> - Supports and resources that ensure student and staff safety and mutual respect
>
> *References;* McCluskey et al. (2008); Varnham (2008); Zehr (1990).

restorative school discipline as a comprehensive approach to primary, secondary, and tertiary prevention for behavioral challenges. Key principles are described, including the focus on relationships; problem solving; the prevention and peaceful resolution of conflict; and strategies for restoration and making amends where harm has occurred. Steps are provided that school leaders can take to prepare their schools for restorative school discipline, and sample information is provided for sharing with the school community. The next chapter describes the process of setting transparent and fair schoolwide behavior expectations as well as ensuring that school rules are culturally responsive to today's diverse school population.

2 Schoolwide Behavior Expectations

This chapter addresses the first tasks confronting school leaders: specifying and communicating behavior expectations for the school community. Nearly every school will have a set of rules or guidelines that encompass expectations for students, but some guidelines will be more meaningful and interpretable than others. You can test how well the current rules and guidelines at your school are working by answering the following question: Can typical students at any grade level in your school state the rules for how to behave in the hallway, restroom, etc.?

Later in the guide, we present a framework for translating "behavior expectations for the school community" into observable behaviors, restorative practices when things have gone wrong, and consequences that will be enforced at school whenever students do not meet behavior expectations. In this chapter, however, it is important to reinforce that *unless you can translate "behavior expectations" into observable behaviors, they will have little meaning for students and are open to abuse by everyone—including school personnel.* Sometimes this will require stating a rule in more behavioral (observable) terms, and sometimes it will require breaking down a word like *appropriate* or *properly* into examples at different ages so that students and adults are clear about what is meant by the rule.

IDENTIFYING SCHOOLWIDE BEHAVIOR EXPECTATIONS

Before young people can be expected to show good behavior in school, they need to have a clear understanding of what the school community expects of them at any particular age and also why. In today's schools, these behavior expectations, or rules, need to be stated clearly for all school settings, including classrooms, hall or walkways, stairs, restrooms, cafeteria, assembly, library, gym/intramural sports facilities, school bus, and outdoor area surrounding the school. A school with transparent rules that are well understood by all students in that school will have fewer difficulties with bullying than one where the principal does not assume agency or perhaps even does not accept responsibility for what happens in the immediate school community. Very general rules such as "no running" appear on virtually every list of school behavioral expectations, but this rule alone doesn't ensure safety on stairways, for example. Especially in big schools where large numbers of students change classrooms regularly throughout the day, a rule such as "no running" may not have as much meaning or be nearly as effective as "walk and pass on the left."

What Are Schoolwide Behavioral Expectations?

Table 1 presents Jarrett Middle School's behavior expectations, which were developed through extensive consultation across the school. Before specifying the school's behavioral expectations, Jarrett staff agreed to feature three broad expectations—caring, responsible, and always learning. In the table, the behaviors to meet each of these expectations are described for different school environments. Does the table include enough information for children—or even for teachers—to know what is acceptable and what is not?

The table indicates that in the restroom children demonstrate *caring* by respecting the privacy of others, using toilets and urinals properly, and waiting for one's turn. To demonstrate *responsible*, they are to keep restrooms clean, conserve supplies, and use the restroom for its intended use. Finally, for *always learning*, they should practice good hygiene, wash hands, and throw rubbish in trash cans. How would a seventh grader interpret "keep restrooms clean"? Certain expectations within each box could be elsewhere in the matrix: perhaps "throw rubbish in trash cans" under *always learning* would fit better in the category *responsible* and may even be an example of "keep restrooms clean."

General expectations such as "keeping [a place] clean" require clarification: we don't expect students to actually clean the restroom, but we do expect them to clean up after themselves and not leave a mess for the next person. While this may appear to be commonsense, it is appropriate in some cultures to squat on the toilet seat, which will leave footprints and a dirty toilet seat for the next person, who may be more likely to sit on the seat. Who communicates with children about these expectations, and how

Table 1 Behavior Expectations at Jarrett Middle School

	All Settings	Stairwell/Walkways	Restrooms	Cafeteria	Assembly	Library	Intramural/Gym
Caring	• Be on time and on task. • Respect the rights and opinions of others. • Work cooperatively. • Use a quiet voice. • Be courteous and patient. • Report any unsafe conditions or students.	• Respect school property. • Be polite and considerate of others.	• Respect privacy of others. • Use toilet and urinals properly. • Wait your turn.	• Be courteous and patient. • Speak quietly. • Keep your place in line.	• Applaud and cheer appropriately. • Be courteous and patient.	• Use a quiet voice. • Be respectful and patient. • Wait in line to be helped.	• Applaud/cheer appropriately. • Be courteous and patient.
Responsible	• Bring required supplies. • Complete assignments on time. • Be prepared for class. • Follow classroom rules. • Make good choices. • Take care of outstanding obligations.	• Practice safe behavior. • Walk and pass on the left • Avoid loitering in stairwell. • Remain on ground floor during noninstructional times. • Keep school environment clean.	• Keep restrooms clean. • Conserve supplies. • Use restroom for its intended use.	• Walk at all times. • Use your own picture ID. • Keep area clean. • Empty trays and milk properly.	• Pay attention to speaker/performer. • Enter/leave in an orderly manner. • Sit in assigned seat. • Keep area clean.	• Return books on time. • Follow library rules and procedures. • Know your AR reading level and user number. • Take care of library materials.	• Follow gym rules. • Enter/leave in an orderly manner. • Take care of and return equipment. • Attend scheduled games.
Always Learning	• Practice appropriate behavior. • Keep on task. • Participate in classroom activities. • Follow directions and all safety rules.	• Practice appropriate behavior. • Use appropriate language.	• Practice good hygiene. • Wash hands. • Throw rubbish in trash cans.	• Practice proper table manners.	• Practice active listening and proper social etiquette.	• Ask for assistance. • Learn to use available/new resources.	• Participate in activity. • Follow instructions and all safety rules.

does this occur? Our schools have increasingly multiethnic student populations, yet their basic structures and systems may be very monocultural—putting some students at ease and challenging others whose culture differs markedly from the dominant mainstream culture. It is easy to forget the extent to which we rely on ongoing socialization to teach children things like "restroom rules" that may not, in fact, be universally understood.

Having clear expectations expressed through observable behaviors is particularly important wherever there is a risk for bullying. Examine Jarrett's list of expectations for the stairwell and walkways: Do they rule out bullying behavior, or would another set of rules be needed to cover instances of bullying? Ideally, these behavior expectations should preclude bullying and not require another layer of rules to prevent behavior problems and abuse. Table 2 illustrates how *caring* can be defined by going beyond generic references to respect for people and property to suggest specific behaviors.

Table 2 Being Specific About How to Demonstrate Caring in the Stairwell/Walkways to Prevent Bullying

	Stairwell/Walkways— General and Nonspecific	Stairwell/Walkways—More Specific and Oriented Toward Antibullying
Caring	• Respect school property. • Be polite and considerate of others.	• Respect school property and report damage. • Invite a classmate who is walking alone to walk with you to the next class. • Ask for help from a teacher if you see someone being bullied.

Developing Your School's Behavior Expectations

To develop a set of behavior expectations for your school, go through the following steps:

Step 1: Identify high level principles for your school expectations such as the ones identified for Jarrett (caring, responsible, always learning). To do this, raise the issue for discussion on the agenda of meetings of your school board, school senior management team, and teacher meetings. In addition, announce at school assembly that students are invited to make suggestions and provide a suggestion box outside the school office for ideas about "Behavior Expectations for [My School]." Identify someone such as an assistant or vice principal or, if your school does not have these, a senior teacher as "project manager" to be in charge of this process. Identify others to work with you and the project manager, including a teacher who has particular interest in care for students, a behavioral support specialist or resource person from your district, and a parent from the school community as a committee to develop the principles. Put the issue on the agenda for the next meeting of each group for discussion to generate ideas and ensure that the project manager attends each meeting and records key ideas and concerns.

Step 2: Convene a meeting of the committee chaired by the project manager and attended by you to review all suggestions put forward by different groups at meetings. Under the leadership of the project manager, list and summarize the suggestions, and propose choices of no more than three to four overall expectations for the school. Using a chart similar to Table 1 for Jarrett, but with the cells blank under each school environment heading, enter the expectations in the far left column.

Step 3: The project manager should take the draft table back to each group listed under Step 1 for discussion, recording carefully what is said about which different observable behaviors demonstrate each expectation. The project manager must guide the discussions so that participants think about what each of the proposed expectations would look like as an observable behavior in the different table cells. It will be helpful to have at least one other member of the working committee present at these meetings—the teacher leader, the behavioral specialist, and the parent—and with you as chair of the meeting to make clear your support for the process.

Step 4: Based on the discussions from Step 3, revise the draft table and prepare a final version for wide distribution across the school community. Put the table of expectations on the agenda for the next available teacher meeting, school board meeting, parent night at the school, and assembly for students. Prepare a flyer including the set of Behavioral Expectations for [Your School Name] for distribution along with a brief rationale and description of the process used to develop them. Give all students a copy of the flyer to take home with them and ensure postings of larger displays of the behavior expectations as appropriate throughout the school.

Ongoing: Review the set of behavior expectations and sample observable behaviors annually to ensure that they reflect ongoing needs, issues, and concerns. The project manager will be in charge of this review and should inform recommendations for changes based on systematic analysis of behavioral issues and incidents throughout the year.

SUMMARY

This chapter provides an overview of procedures to develop schoolwide behavior expectations that are realistic for children across the ages represented in the school population. The processes described here are designed to ensure full school involvement in the development of a transparent set of schoolwide behavior expectations that can be judged fair and reasonable.

Section II

Putting the Model in Place

3 Processes for Primary Prevention and Intervention

The first section of this chapter describes the specific schoolwide processes that are used for prevention and peaceful resolution of conflict, and that build on a restorative culture. The school leader's role includes: (a) supporting teachers' use of restorative practices *curricula* across the grades such as restorative language and scripts, restorative inquiry, restorative conversations, and use of meetings and conferences; (b) setting up systems for mediation, shuttle mediation, and peer mediation; and (c) establishing guidelines and procedures for formal conferences for serious offenses as part of a restorative school discipline framework. This chapter also addresses cultural issues and processes for ensuring positive relationships with children and families from cultural and linguistic backgrounds (often referred to as *culturally and linguistically diverse* or CLD in the special education literature) that differ from the dominant school culture. Chapter 4 addresses the framework for child-focused interventions, but this chapter provides an overview of team and organizational networks likely to be part of the process of developing and evaluating these interventions. The chapter concludes with a section on how school leaders can address children's achievement, mental health, socioemotional, and social friendship needs in school through strategies such as mentoring and peer support.

PREVENTION: RESTORATIVE SCHOOL DISCIPLINE STRUCTURES AND PROCESSES

Restorative school discipline begins fundamentally in the classroom. Classroom climate reflects the teaching and learning relationships of the teacher with children and that of children with one another. A positive classroom climate requires an emotionally intelligent teacher who *assumes agency* for student learning. Advocating that teachers need to *accept responsibility* for student outcomes can be regarded as a criticism that somehow they are refusing to do something expected of them. We prefer the term *agency* over *responsibility* to signal a more proactive role whereby the teacher commits to enhancing every child's learning and behavior, including those children who come to school with multiple challenges in their lives.

The focus on supporting and repairing relationships in the classroom acknowledges the importance of a safe and nurturing context for learning and positive behavior. Students cannot learn effectively in an environment where they are disrespected and socially excluded (Evans & Harvey, 2012). Restorative practices acknowledge that conflict may have led to broken relationships and ongoing negative social interactions. What must happen next is to restore positive interactions and good relationships while also making amends following conflict that has caused harm. Thus, the first step has to be ensuring that the culture of the school and every classroom supports the peaceful resolution of conflict—which is perhaps inevitable in any human environment—and enables children to make restitution without losing dignity and respect.

This section of *The School Leader's Guide* provides an overview of classroom-level processes for restorative curricula, mediation, and restorative meeting and conferencing that are essential for restorative practices at both the school and classroom level. Details of those components designed for implementation in classrooms by teachers are included in *The Teacher's Guide to Restorative Classroom Discipline* (2012), and the information included here is designed to provide the principal with sufficient background to oversee and support these practices across the school. In addition, Chapter 6 includes details for the principal about how to establish the formal conferencing procedures for restorative approaches for serious incidents that might otherwise lead to punitive-only consequences, including suspension and exclusion.

Restorative Curricula

Classroom teachers committed to restorative practices have developed authentic caring relationships with their students (Valenzuela, 1999).

Authentic caring entails taking responsibility for creating a classroom environment that enables students to learn. It affirms the multiple "funds of knowledge" (Gonzalez, Moll, & Amanti, 2005) that students bring to the classroom as valued identities from their home communities, and it means getting to know students as learners. Aesthetic caring refers to only affective expressions, showing students that you like and care about them as persons. Authentic caring does the same but goes further in encompassing "warm demander pedagogy" associated with effective, culturally responsive teaching (Ware, 2006). Aesthetic carers can be overly accepting of behavior that reflects low expectations and poor achievement, whereas authentic caring involves high expectations and conditions that lead to enhanced achievement.

Classroom implementation typically involves a series of lessons or activities designed for all students rather than being focused solely on children who exhibit challenging behavior or being reactive in response to incidents. In these whole-class activities, teachers ask students to consider challenging issues: they might, for example, ask students to discuss a newspaper feature about a recent local incident involving charges of racism, or they could discuss a media report of text bullying. The focus of these discussions is to practice using *restorative language and scripts* (see below) that illuminate the importance of understanding events and their impact on the people involved.

A Generic Restorative Script

- What happened?
- What do you think about what happened?
- What might someone else think about what happened?
- Who has been affected by what happened?
- In what way?
- What do you think has to happen next to make things better?

As teachers become more experienced in using the script, they will develop the skills needed to vary the questions to fit particular events and circumstances. They will also be able to adapt this basic script to fit children's language and culture.

In addition to using a semiformal script like this in group discussions with students, teachers engage in and thus model active nonjudgmental listening skills toward developing those skills in children as well. We often leap to interpretations that fit our preconceived ideas about people and events, failing to hear people out and listen to information that would give us a far clearer and more accurate picture of what happened. In addition, listening carefully to someone—whether that person is another professional or a child—communicates fundamental respect to the person, just as failing to hear the other side of the story shuts people down and communicates a kind of righteous assertion of a power imbalance. The following examples illustrate restorative language that teachers can use to initiate discussion of an incident or challenge:

- Can someone tell me what happened?
- Can I tell you what happened from my perspective? Does anyone else see it differently?
- How do you feel about that?
- Could you each tell me how you see things? Let's have XXXX go first and after she has finished, XXXX can give his perspective. After both of you have explained what happened, we can try to sort this out.

In these kinds of conversations, the teacher takes a neutral perspective and tries to support students to identify on their own what needs to be done to either put things right or move on if the problem cannot be solved just then. School personnel should be prepared to use this nonconfrontational conversation anywhere, for example, in the school lunchroom if there has been a negative interaction between students.

Mediation

The restorative script described above is informal mediation: individuals or groups are being asked to consider the cause of an incident and also different perspectives on that incident with a view toward reaching consensus on how to move forward. However, these informal conversations may not be sufficient for conflict in many situations, particularly when it is obvious that different participants in a conflict situation are miles apart in their perceptions of the incident and what needs to happen next. Where conflict has caused harm or whenever both parties feel strongly that the other person is the cause of the problem, formal mediation will be needed. Mediation is a process in which those involved in conflict are supported by a neutral third party—the mediator—who supports them to hear different perspectives and find a mutually acceptable way forward (Kane et al., 2007). Mediation differs from the more typical process of having a designated authority figure who metes out justice when an offender is sent to the office by a teacher or other school staff member. In mediation, those who are involved in the conflict are viewed as being in the best position to identify ways to resolve that conflict, make amends for any harm caused, and resolve how to move forward. Thus, *the offender* and *the offended* are part of the mediation process. Evaluation is an important part of the mediation process. Whenever a mediation system is in place, there should be a procedure for logging incidents so that the school can evaluate whether the mediation initiative is having a positive impact, no effect, or might even be associated with an increase in incidents.

Peer mediation

In schools, the mediator is likely to be a teacher or someone who provides support services such as a school counselor or a deputy principal. However, middle and high school students are mature enough to be trained to carry out peer mediation, particularly where there is a strong school culture of informal conferencing and restorative scripts operating in classrooms across the school years. Peer mediation could be expected on the playground, for example, at recess and lunchtime with some less formal support from school personnel assigned to supervise at that time. Peer mediators could be older peers who volunteer to mediate conflict involving younger students on the playground under the watchful eye of the adult supervisor. Organizing a peer mediation system for nonclassroom settings could be a productive activity for a school's home-school partnership program that could organize and run buddy restorative workshops for all students (Kane et al., 2007). Ongoing records must be kept for playground accidents, post-recess referrals, and "on-the-fence" (i.e., students lined up along the playground fence for the remainder of recess as punishment) discipline-type consequences for conflict. These records are examined to determine whether such discipline incidents are decreasing in frequency and/or intensity in association with informal mediation networks such as these operating on the playground.

The selection of peer mediators is important. Schools may identify peer mediators by student applications, student nominations, or teacher nominations. Often, these processes result in identifying students as mediators who are considered to be exemplary and school leaders (Algozzine, Daunic, & Smith, 2010). The problem with this approach is an issue of credibility and relevance for the students who are referred as offenders. Undoubtedly, student leaders are selected as top students who exhibit teacher-like characteristics such as being responsible and self-managing. As student leaders, however, top students may be quite unlike students referred for mediation who may be disengaged and even hostile to the school.

For mediation to work, it must be socially acceptable to all participants— including the student who is referred for problem behavior (Robinson, Smith, & Daunic, 2000). Blake, Wang, Cartledge, and Gardner (2000) demonstrated that students who had a history of behavioral problems can be trained to be effective trainers in teaching social skills to others. Algozinne and his colleagues (2010) suggest that peer mediators who themselves have shown high levels of interpersonal conflict at school "have the potential to become peer mediators and, in so doing, enhance a program's overall acceptability" (p. 120). In addition, cultural factors should be considered in identifying particular peer mediators for a given situation: whenever possible, peer mediators should share cultural understandings with the offender and any student victims.

Shuttle mediation

Shuttle mediation is a term describing situations where at least one of the parties involved in a conflict is afraid, unwilling, or unable to meet face-to-face with others who are involved. In shuttle mediation, the mediator moves back and forth between those involved in the conflict. The mediator might first listen to the student's side of the story, then hear what the teacher has to say, then go back to the student to discuss what the teacher said, then go back to the teacher to discuss what the student said, and so on.

Mentoring

Mentoring is another widely used approach for supporting students who are judged at risk for or who already exhibit some initial behavioral and educational difficulties. This section provides basic information on what mentoring is and what the research literature tells us about what can and cannot be achieved through mentoring. Mentoring programs are not particularly effective in dealing with young people who have already engaged in serious antisocial and illegal acts or who have socioemotional difficulties as a result of physical or sexual abuse. Mentoring can be extremely valuable as a prevention program, particularly for young people who have limited access to effective adult role models, and mentors may also be extremely helpful as potential mediators for interventions if carefully structured.

As with mediation, the personal characteristics of the mentor in relationship to the characteristics of children and youth being mentored can be crucial for effectiveness. For example, sometimes the life circumstances and history of the mentor bear no resemblance to those of the child, as is the case when an older, white, and relatively wealthy adult mentors an African American teenager from a low-income family. In cases such as this one, mentoring could actually result in resentment by the child (and/or the family) and unrealistic expectations, rather than the intended help to develop personal characteristics through modeling likely to lead to constructive behavior in the future. To anticipate and avoid such possible negative outcomes, potential mentors have to be made aware that it is the nature of the relationship between the mentor and the mentee that is so crucial. There is no evidence that cross-race matches are less successful than same-race matches—what is important is consideration of the mentee's developmental stage, general interests, and the support and supervision provided to the mentor.

Local organizations such as Rotary or the YMCA may offer valuable resources such as camps, afterschool programs, and other enrichment programs in addition to mentoring opportunities. Such programs are popular ways of managing challenging youngsters, but the expectations need to be carefully assessed. An outdoor adventure program, however exciting it may sound, cannot in a few days of even intense experiences overcome many years of inappropriate learning or absence of emotional skill development. The same argument can be presented with respect to other popular but much more authoritarian programs that policy makers tend to advocate, such as "scared straight" (which involve visits to prisons to see firsthand how bad such an experience can be), or military-style "boot camps," which research evidence suggests are harmful, not simply ineffective.

Sometimes school leaders are encouraged by well-meaning school boards or district superintendents to set up or support programs that are supposed to challenge young people, boost their self-esteem, bring famous sporting stars to the campus, or attempt to set students on a moral pathway (such as "just saying 'no' to sex and drugs"). Before agreeing to implement such a program, it is important to ask for any evaluation information the program might have. This does not need to be controlled research, but any legitimate program will have information on such issues as (a) acceptability of the program to young people (e.g., dropout rates versus completion); (b) acceptability to parents; (c) the professional qualifications of those conducting the program; (d) the motivation behind the organizers and developers of the program (financial gain, feeling good, conversion to a faith—these are not necessarily bad, you just need to know about them); and (e) some indication of program *integrity* (that is to say, the degree to which the actual program follows the principles and practices outlined in the program descriptions). Another useful strategy for avoiding mistakes or being disappointed is to collaborate closely with a national organization with impeccable credentials: Big Brothers/Big Sisters of America being an excellent example.

Setting up a mentoring program in my school community

Any intervention can have unintended side effects, referred to as *iatrogenic effects* when they cause harm or make matters worse. Mentors can actually have a negative influence if they are not carefully chosen and engage in antisocial rather than prosocial behavior with the student being mentored. To protect against possible negative effects, a new mentoring program should follow the very clear guidelines that have been established based on many research studies that have evaluated the effectiveness of mentoring. One of the most important things to remember is that the research evidence suggests only modest benefits from young people participating in such programs. As explained, it is at-risk young people from disadvantaged backgrounds who are most likely to benefit from participation, as opposed to youth who already engage in serious delinquent activities. One of the best resources, freely available on the Internet, has been developed by the Hamilton Fish Institute on School and Community Violence (2007). In particular, we suggest using their checklist of mentoring program progress, provided on pages 91 to 95 of their guide to mentoring.

If the following issues and principles are adhered to, a school is likely to be able to conduct a successful mentoring program:

1. Effective mentoring programs start with a warm, close relationship between a caring adult and the young person being mentored; however, that alone is not sufficient. Successful programs do not rely exclusively on the relationship: the mentoring is just one component of a focused effort to enhance youth development, such as a homework support project, academic tutoring, study skills development, or life skills training.

2. Successful programs always provide intensive peer supervision for the mentors, with clear guidelines around such criteria as the frequency of contact (at least once a week is expected), the expected duration of the relationship, and so on. Mentoring relationships should last at least one year; short-term relationships can be harmful. Even if the mentoring program is a volunteer activity provided by the community, the school must take ownership by, for example, having an experienced senior teacher from the school be a manager, establishing requirements such as police checks, and actively participating in the selection of suitable student mentees.

3. When schools take ownership of mentoring programs, they maintain data that will guide the programs and evaluate effectiveness. The school will take responsibility for monitoring: improved grades, reduced unexcused absences, student and parent satisfaction, and fewer disciplinary incidents. However, if someone in your school or local community wishes to start a mentoring program, it is usually more beneficial to form a collaboration with an already established or national mentoring program.

4. Successful mentors are positive role models, able to establish a warm relationship and alert to the need to establish some boundaries. They do not undermine the primary role of the parent. The school's commitment to a mentoring program is revealed when a significant number of teachers volunteer to be mentors in the program. Teacher mentors are particularly valuable in enhancing home-school communication.

5. With school-based mentoring programs, there needs to be a large menu of possible structured activities, both within the school, after normal hours, and outside the school, accessing community resources. However, unstructured, fun, interesting activities that take the mentee outside his or her usual range of experiences should occur in equal measure.

6. Having specified goals is valuable, but they should be realistic. The major goal for any program should be raising academic achievement and increasing the young person's engagement with the school. Reducing antisocial behavior can be expected to a degree. With older students, preparing them for the world of work or interesting them in college is a viable and important goal. Mentors' expectations need to be adjusted according to the developmental level and requirements of the mentee.

7. Programs also need to be fun and appealing to young people. Successful mentoring programs encourage choice and are not overly prescriptive. Working on psychological and interpersonal goals is likely to be more informal and engaging for young people.

8. Effective programs actively involve families. A parent or guardian needs to know exactly who the mentor is, what his or her background has been, and what sorts of activities are likely to occur. And, of course, a parent is also a useful source of information regarding the young person: what are her interests, special needs, religious faith, allergies (all the sort of personal information that a mentor needs to know and that you in the school may not be aware of).

Bullying

Bullying can be identified when a student is the target of any behavior that is harmful or intended to be harmful, is repeated regularly or occurs over a period of time, and involves an imbalance of power such that the victim does not feel that he or she can stop the interaction (Olweus, 2001). Such negative behavior can take a variety of forms, some direct, such as physical or verbal attacks, and some indirect, such excluding someone or spreading rumors. Bullying at school creates a multitude of direct and indirect problems, to the most extreme outcomes such as its link to one possible cause of teen suicide. While this may sound extreme, surveys reveal that middle school-aged students rank being physically or emotionally bullied by other children as one of the worst things that could happen to them (e.g., Maxwell & Carroll-Lind, 1997). This section draws on the literature in providing information about effective antibullying models and approaches (as there is more than one).

Bullying, as an unwanted component of school life, is connected to our general topic of challenging behavior in a number of ways. First, it links to our overarching principle of restorative justice. This is because more conventional punitive models of school discipline simply replicate the bullying ethos: some difficult students are targeted repeatedly for punishment, and others are rejected from the mainstream group, through home detention, exclusion, and expulsion. Second, there is very clear evidence that a bullying problem in a school reflects a negative school climate—it is a barometer of the degree to which the school has a positive atmosphere that reflects values of caring, justice, safety, and equitable treatment for all. Bullies report feeling significantly alienated from school and less comfortable in the school environment. Third, many of the students exhibiting the behavior problems we are concerned about are either themselves bullies or victims of bullies. It will come as no surprise that students identified as bullies during their elementary years are four times more likely to become delinquent teenagers and have criminal convictions in adulthood (Olweus, 1993). What might be less obvious, however, is that the *victims* of bullying are affected, not just in terms of academic work, but in their socioemotional development as well. The phenomenon of the "aggressive victim," first described by Olweus, is now quite well understood (Schwartz, Dodge, Pettit, & Bates, 1997). While it is true that many victims of bullying are passive (pervasively submissive), there is a distinct subgroup of victims who themselves are, or become, very physically aggressive. Since victims of bullying do not always report it, when a student is identified as engaging in aggressive and violent behavior, the possibility that he or she is a victim of bullying must always be entertained and investigated.

The fact that bullying is often not reported by the victims presents a real challenge for school leaders. In one large anonymous survey of student in middle school, about one third of them indicated they had experienced bullying (Unnever & Cornell, 2004). Twenty-five percent of that group had not told anyone, and 40% had not told an adult. In our own experience of talking to elementary school students about their educational experiences, many of them pointed out that although teachers were strongly opposed to bullying, the worst offenders did not do it in the presence of teachers. When students tried to report an incidence of bullying, quite a few teachers told them to deal with bullying themselves, and parents can also be prone to recommend that if their children encounter bullying, they need to learn to hit back. This may explain why children who report that their parents use coercive disciplinary practices are unlikely to tell their parents that they are being bullied. Thus, principals often genuinely believe that they do not have a bullying problem in their school, until a serious incident gets media attention, when it is no longer possible to deny the problem.

A good example of a complex bullying problem is what happens on school buses where the only adult observer is often the driver who is preoccupied with safe driving. Another complex feature of expectations around bullying relate to cyberbullying using cell phones, text messages, cell-phone cameras, and web postings of various kinds. Expectations around such behaviors will be entirely different at the high school level, where in some cases low-level bullying may be so endemic that the teenage students are not always aware of the acceptable standards of response—these will need to be understood and communicated by the principal.

Identifying bullying

To address bullying effectively, school personnel and students must acknowledge that some interpersonal interactions may not immediately look like conflict but are in fact low-intensity levels of bullying that lead to harm. People often convince themselves that humor generally and teasing specifically are innocent behaviors that may even be seen as clever rather than damaging: you may hear someone being urged to "Have a sense of humor" or be told that "We were only teasing." Humor is an important part of human interactions, and there is evidence that one characteristic of good teachers is being able to use humor effectively in teaching and learning interactions. But humor that comes at the expense of another person, makes fun of someone, and highlights personal characteristics that can make the other person feel bad is destructive and signals a pattern of bullying. Students and staff must be able to recognize teasing that has gone beyond "good fun," which can easily be identified through observation of who is laughing—the teaser or the teased? A first step to preventing and addressing bullying in any school is building understandings about bullying as a continuum of behavior that is disrespectful and insensitive to the feelings of others.

The activity in Table 3, focused on a continuum of bullying, can help staff and students acknowledge and remediate problematic exchanges. Elementary teachers could use this activity format in the classroom by filling in only one or two examples of common interactions seen at a particular grade level, then asking the children to fill in other examples and talk about the examples using this format as part of class conferencing. The principal can also use the format at a staff meeting to identify endemic problems and possible bullying occurring in hallways, the cafeteria, and other common areas at school and then to launch a schoolwide effort to prevent and intervene with bullying. Of course, a most important part of any such effort is not just identifying bullying and telling everyone not to do things but building interventions that are age appropriate and doable for the bully, the victim, and bystanders or observers of bullying.

Table 3 Activity Focused on a Continuum of Bullying

Discuss the behaviors described below and explain why these are examples of bullying and how you can identify if they are doing harm to others.

The Behavior	When This is Bullying	How Can You Tell?
Teacher singles out a student who is late to class by saying loudly, "So, you came late to try to avoid the science experiment?"		
Student tells another student on the bus to move to another seat because he prefers that seat.		
A group of students laugh at the answer given by a classmate who didn't understand the teacher's question.		
A teenager receives a series of text messages commenting on her physical appearance.		
A student in first grade is told by two other boys playing a game at recess that he cannot play with them.		

Preventing and intervening with bullying

The first step to preventing bullying in school is to have a proactive approach in place. Prevention requires that students have ongoing opportunities to develop strategies for conflict resolution, peer mediation, and response to threats and dangerous situations in ways that protect and defuse rather than react helplessly or escalate the danger. Conflict Resolution Education (CRE) is an evidence-based approach that teaches students constructive conflict management so that the entire school becomes an environment where teachers and students alike take responsibility for a positive school climate (Garrard & Lipsey, 2007). CRE programs are implemented in the classroom by teachers to facilitate constructive and peaceful resolution of interpersonal conflicts. CRE curricula work to shift win-lose situations to win-win solutions by using conflict in positive ways as opportunities to develop children's skills in empathic listening, anger management, bias awareness, social skills, negotiation, and group problem solving (Daunic, Smith, Robinson, Miller, & Landry, 2000). Regular use of cooperative learning strategies by teachers provides a positive context for increasing students' interpersonal skills and understandings. These approaches should begin at school entry so that by the time students reach middle school—when peer conflict is particularly salient as well as hurtful—they are equipped with the social skills to prevent bullying and avoid engaging in incidents that evolve into bullying. A recent Cochrane review[1] of school-based programs for preventing violence (Mytton, DiGuiseppi, Gough, Taylor, & Logan, 2006) concluded that programs designed simply to teach other students not to respond with anger to provocation, aggression, or violence were not, in fact, very effective. Better outcomes were reported for interventions designed to improve relationships among peers and to increase students' social skills, such as empathy.

Specific bullying intervention programs typically focus on the bully or the victim, or both. They mesh well with CRE approaches, but bullying interventions are better suited to adult mediation rather than peer mediation given that bullying is characterized by peer conflict and peer power relationships. The first step in any antibullying program is to have agreed processes in place for children to report bullying incidents to a trusted adult—a teacher, counselor, or other staff member at school—without risk to their psychological or physical safety. This requires some discussion

---

[1]Cochrane reviews are systematic reviews of a given area of research that follow scholarly guidelines specified by the Cochrane Collaboration. Although originally designed to provide evidence for medical treatments, there are now many Cochrane reviews in the social sciences and in education. Free access is available at www2.cochrane.org/reviews/.

among staff, since, as we have pointed out, bullying doesn't generally occur in the presence of adults but in places where adult supervision is less evident, such as on the playground or school bus or in the cafeteria or hallways. The trusted adult selected for this role must make a commitment to explore the incident, never to doubt the accuracy of the victim's report, never to suggest that the victim deal with it on his or her own, and to follow up on the incident without indicating who complained. None of these conditions can be assumed to be ingrained in all staff, since staff attitudes toward bullying vary greatly. One reason for this is that teachers themselves may have been bullied when students or may themselves be guilty of bullying styles of behavior toward students or even other staff. Just as teachers occasionally have pet students, so they sometimes have students they pick on, sometimes under the guise of good-natured teasing. Student themselves often report that teachers seem to have it in for certain students to whom they have taken a dislike—for example, Russell Bishop's interviews with minority teenagers from an indigenous culture revealed that students were well aware of certain peers being picked on unfairly (Bishop & Berryman, 2006). Also, workplace bullying is far from uncommon, and it is possible that some teachers in a school will feel some degree of bullying from more senior, powerful, or dominant fellow teachers, all of which points to the value of monitoring school climate by asking teachers what their impressions are of the working atmosphere that they experience.

Finally, when ensuring that all staff without exception are committed to the elimination of bullying, it is important for older teachers, less familiar with modern technology available to youth, to recognize not only how widespread cyberbullying is but also how viscious and destructive it can be. Staff across the school must acknowledge that bullying takes various forms: physical violence may be easier to recognize, but malicious gossip or texts and social exclusion from play groups at recess are also forms of bullying that cause emotional harm.

The Olweus Bullying Prevention Program is well known and has undergone more than two decades of research on its effectiveness and adaptability to different educational contexts (Bauer, Lozano, & Rivara, 2007; Olweus, 2003). The approach builds on a set of key principles for the school environment that are consistent with the restorative school discipline approach: (1) adults must show warmth toward and interest in students; (2) there are consistent expectations for prosocial behavior; (3) violations of expectations are met with restorative, not punitive, consequences; and (4) adults in the school act as role models for nonbullying interactions with one another and with children. We recommend that school leaders work with the advice of specialist behavioral consultants such as the school psychologist before adopting or adapting a schoolwide approach to bullying. Behavioral specialists working in your district will also have knowledge of other program efforts in the region along with resources available, which can provide schools with valuable networking and peer support for problem solving.

RESTORATIVE CONFERENCING

School leaders play a key role in supporting restorative practices at the classroom level and across the school setting outside the school classroom. These less formal and ongoing restorative practices are the responsibility of all school personnel. In contrast, the school principal in particular has a special responsibility for *restorative conferencing* at school level. A restorative conference is a formal meeting of those who are directly involved in a particular incident in which harm has been caused or perceived as being imminent. Those who should be included in the conference are the student(s) who are the offender(s), those who are the victims, a trained facilitator (e.g., the principal, dean, or school psychologist), and the teachers, peers, family members, and other concerned parties.

As serious misbehavior involving assault, property damage (e.g., fire setting), and drug use is likely to come to the attention of the local juvenile justice system, it is very valuable to ensure that relevant community police officers are involved as well. Almost all police departments have specially trained youth aid officers (sometimes referred to as the *juvenile division*); their focus is inevitably on prevention and ensuring that first offenders do not become repeat offenders. School principals should have a working liaison system with the senior youth aid officers in their district so that agreements can be reached *before* a serious incident occurs, regarding the philosophies, expectations, and legal requirements under which the school and the juvenile justice system operate. Some police departments have school resource officers assigned to the school. These individuals not only ensure good open communication with the school administration, but they also conduct local and national educational programs designed to keep the school safe and drug and violence free. Another common strategy in many communities is to have youth aid panels. These operate under principles very similar to restorative justice ideas. The panels are made up of community volunteers, screened by the police department, and trained by the juvenile court. The volunteers represent the ethnic, cultural, gender, and economic diversity of the district; they are not a court of law and do not determine guilt or innocence. Therefore, it is usually required that the young person has admitted to the offense, and the panel's task is to suggest constructive solutions that will circumvent the more formal processes involved in juvenile court.

When Is a Restorative Conference Needed?

The need for a formal restorative conference is signaled by the nature of the incident and serious behavior that may result in consequences for the offender such as in-school suspension. The important point is that the conference is crucial, and any consequences do not replace the need for restoration conferencing. A restorative conference may also be a school-wide response to a challenging schoolwide issue, such as bullying that has become widespread in the school restrooms, corridors, and other school environments outside the classroom. Finally, a restorative conference can be focused on a particular student for whom a more intensive intervention is being considered following a series of actions that are not working for that student.

What Should Be the Goal of a Restorative Conference?

The major goal and purpose of the conference is to achieve consensus about the nature of the problem and gather ideas about what actions can be taken for making amends in a manner that allows participants to move forward in a positive way. A viable conference process includes attention to each of the following issues:

- Providing the victim(s) with a voice and meeting the needs of victims.
- Ensuring that the views of all those who are involved in an incident are heard and respected.
- Establishing a process that builds on a restorative ethos—consequences may follow particular behaviors, but these are part of a restorative process not used as punishment as an end goal in itself.

The restorative conference is not about blaming, nor is it about forgiveness or denying harm that may have occurred. Rather, the challenge is to keep the conversation respectful of the dignity of everyone involved. Without great care, a group meeting can quickly become a kind of public retribution in which group participants may gang up on an offender or even a victim so that the activity adds to harm. Hence, the meeting must be facilitated by either the school principal or school psychologist who follows careful guidelines for restoration rather than retribution.

Who Should Facilitate
the Restorative Conference?

A restorative conference can be facilitated successfully by a school psychologist, counselor, deputy principal, dean, or a respected member of the community. In small schools, it may be desirable for the principal to serve as facilitator for some or even all restorative conferences. Criteria for who can serve as the facilitator include identifying someone who (a) is not directly involved in an incident so is more likely to be seen as a neutral party; (b) has the authority within the school and community to invite relevant parties and to follow through to ensure that plans that are developed will be implemented and evaluated; and (c) has undertaken the required study and practice in restorative conferencing for effective facilitation according to restorative practices. Ideally, the school would have a minimum of two trained facilitators who are committed to the process, one of whom might be external to the school (e.g., a community support person) but available on contract when needed. (Details regarding training of restorative conference facilitators are included in *The Consultant's Handbook* in this series.)

Administrative Support for Restorative Conferences

An important reason why the principal assumes special responsibility for the conduct of restorative conferences is that various provisions must be made. There are scheduling considerations, including school staff, family, and student time commitments: a restorative conference may require release time for school personnel or either payment or *time in lieu* for conferences held outside normal school time. Arrangements need to be made to ensure safe transportation for all participants, and some funds may be needed to provide food and drink at the start of the conference. If a community support person who is trained and who can be on call for restorative conferencing is identified, this service can be budgeted at an hourly rate, and the school might budget on the basis that there will be between five to 10 such conferences in a typical school year. Fewer than this number suggests that a school is not taking on restorative practices at a school level, and a higher number—especially at smaller schools—may indicate that incidents are being allowed to escalate rather than being addressed through restorative practices in classrooms throughout the school. In addition, schoolwide use of restorative conferencing should be integrated within the regional or districtwide services available to individual schools with specialist behavioral support as might be provided by a school psychologist. Even where a specially trained facilitator is used for a school's restorative conferencing rather than the school psychologist performing this role, the school's behavioral specialist should be kept informed and even directly involved in particular conferences. For example, the school psychologist's support will be especially helpful in planning a schoolwide response to bullying and also for planning focused on a specific child whose behavior has not responded to systems already in place at the school. The next chapter addresses this issue in more detail where services to individual children are part of the planning.

HOME–SCHOOL INTERACTIONS AND RELATIONSHIPS WITH FAMILIES

The relationship of a school with its community sets the tone for restorative school discipline at every level. The starting point is ensuring that children's families are aware of the school commitment to restorative practices and positive discipline approaches, and these general communication issues are discussed in Chapter 1. When communications are going well with families and parents generally, addressing individual issues will be easier, and there will be less scope for misunderstandings and mistrust. Often, however, a parent's first real interaction with various school personnel will be because an incident has occurred, and the approach by the school can feel quite adversarial to family members even when this is not the intention. Parents may feel that they are being blamed and are expected to solve major issues that they themselves are struggling with. They may feel culturally alienated from the dominant school culture, may speak a first language other than English, be influenced by their own childhood experiences with school, and are generally susceptible to mistrust that puts them on the defensive from the moment of that first contact (Evans, Cicchelli, Cohen, & Shapiro, 1995; Evans, Okifuji, Engler, Bromley, & Tishelman, 1993). Ideally, a behavioral incident won't be the first contact, as schools succeed in establishing positive communications with every child's parents. But where this is not the case for a specific family expected to become involved on behalf of a student who has caused harm, school leaders still have considerable scope for influencing the process of family involvement in a positive way.

Harry (2008) discusses the issue of cultural and linguistic mismatches between the families of children receiving special education services and educational personnel. She highlights how special education requirements and systems are reflective of dominant culture values, including being highly formal, requiring extensive legal and written documents, and working best for highly educated parents who speak English as their first language. In New Zealand, specialist professionals working with indigenous Māori students and their families are expected to take the time to get to know the family on neutral turf and show interest in the family's perspective on the issues (Savage, 2009). Glynn, Berryman, Bidois, and Atvars (1997) describe a process for initiating a student, teacher, and family partnership in behavioral interventions. The process begins not with a formal meeting to discuss the problem but by inviting family members to visit the school and observe a particular cultural event of interest to them: of course, this process won't work if the school is not supporting any such events reflecting the different cultural constituents within the school population. Parents, teachers, and the students themselves are then invited to complete parallel checklists that ask them to respond to three questions:

1. What are problem contexts for students at home and at school?

2. What specific behaviors bother us at home and at school?

3. What are the behaviors we like to see at home or school?

The lists were done independently, and the three lists were collated to identify areas of agreement and disagreement that could be discussed by everyone.

Interestingly, the process identified factors that do have serious intervention implications. Students were the only ones to identify the school bus and being out with friends as problem contexts; school staff were the only ones to identify the lunchroom and school field trips as problem contexts; and parents were the only ones to mention getting up as a problem context. Everyone named homework as a problem context. For problem behaviors, there was agreement that teasing/taunting, shouting/yelling, not listening, and following instructions were problems, but teachers alone mentioned bullying, and only parents mentioned tantrums. For most valued behaviors, all three groups named caring, sharing, good personal care, and being responsible. Family members and students agreed that choosing friends carefully was valued, and students and teachers agreed that listening, supporting, and playing together were valued. Only students mentioned being on time; only teachers mentioned getting involved; and only family members mentioned showing respect for one's own and other people's things.

This process allows the main participants—students, teachers, and family members—to identify the behaviors and contexts that are important and/or challenging to them. Having this information prior to a meeting to discuss an incident might enable participants at that meeting to engage in problem solving more constructively as they would know about areas of shared values as well as areas of agreement. Traditional processes are more likely to foreground only one perspective—usually that of school personnel—to drive intervention planning. If only one perspective is legitimized, the other participants are disempowered and likely to resist assuming agency and taking responsibility for the intervention.

School leaders can encourage teachers to use a process such as this to identify for themselves and also find out from their students and families what they see as valued behavior, problematic behavior, and situations that put them at risk. Teachers can then discuss areas of agreement and disagreement toward understanding different perspectives rather than with a view toward forcing new lists reflecting only agreement. Principals could also use this as a strategy for the school's senior leadership team, teachers, and students to identify the starting point for launching an anti-bullying initiative or a framework for positive teacher-parent conferencing. The strategy can be particularly effective as a starting point for individual conferencing with family members on behalf of students whose behavior signals the need for secondary or tertiary level interventions.

CULTURALLY RESPONSIVE SCHOOLS AND CLASSROOMS

Culturally and linguistically diverse (CLD) students are at increased risk in mainstream schools that are not really so much mainstream as they are reflective of one dominant culture such as the culture of those who are of Western European descent. Despite massive changes in the demographic characteristics of students, the structure of schools hasn't changed a great deal for many decades. Students who speak English as an alternative—not first—language, and students who are immigrants or even refugees from conflict regions internationally now populate schools in countries such as the United States, Britain, Germany, Australia, Canada, and New Zealand in ever-increasing numbers. In many urban schools in the United States and Britain, the majority of the student population is not descended from Western European ancestors but instead encompasses diverse cultural groups including African, Hispanic, Asian, Pacific Island, and Eastern European descendants. Nations such as the United States and Australia also have indigenous peoples whose presence predates the colonial settlers who later established schools characterized by teaching and learning that to this day reflect Western organizational structures and curricula. Individualistic and competitive models of schooling are quite unlike the collectivist values and practices of indigenous peoples in particular, resulting in cultural mismatches between school achievement expectations and community perspectives (Castagno & Brayboy, 2008). The majority of school leaders are well aware of these issues in today's schools, but there may be individual teachers and other school personnel whose experiences and expectations have remained quite traditional—and hence somewhat dysfunctional in diverse contexts.

It is a well-established fact that CLD learners are disproportionately referred for special education services, labeled as having disabilities such as emotional disturbance and behavioral disorders, and suspended and excluded from school for behavior (Cartledge & Kourea, 2008; Skiba et al., 2008). These disproportions reflect cultural mainstreams that advantage children who match that mainstream—those who are white and middle class—and disadvantage children whose cultural and linguistic identities are different and hence "minoritized" by the identity of the school (Shields, Bishop, & Mazawi, 2005). Cultural differences can have particular consequences for judgments about behavior. What is inappropriate for one cultural identity may be quite normal for another. Whenever schools are setting general behavioral expectations, it is important to seek advice from community constituents who are knowledgeable about the mores of different cultural groups represented in the school. There may be some teachers whose cultural and linguistic identity matches that of some of the students, but teachers may have themselves become so acculturated to the school's dominant mainstream culture that they are actually no longer in tune with important cultural differences. Key community stakeholders will be an important source of advice for the school principal.

A particular risk for minoritized cultures is that schools and professionals will come to view children and their families from CLD groups as having *deficits* rather than recognizing cultural differences. A child may be seen entirely from a *deficit theorizing perspective* when in fact that student is simply displaying typical behaviors that are encouraged and valued outside school. Deficit perspectives can also mean that dominant culture professionals see only the student's deficits or weaknesses, ignoring and perhaps not even knowing about the student's strengths. Cultural advice can be a critical component in school and individualized planning where there are behavioral conflicts. Many years ago, Sue (1998) emphasized the need for professionals to develop "cultural competence" so that they would be able to interact with those from different cultural groups. Part of being culturally competent is actually recognizing that because one doesn't know enough about another cultural perspective, cultural advice is needed.

Currently, there is a growing literature on culturally responsive schooling and pedagogy to guide educators in the process of becoming culturally competent (Gay, 2010; Sleeter & Grant, 2009; Sleeter, 2011). School leaders play a key role in being aware of this literature and communicating expectations that the professional school community receives the necessary professional development to ensure that cultural mismatches do not unfairly disadvantage and discriminate against children and their families.

SUMMARY

This chapter describes schoolwide processes that, once well established, can prevent conflict and intervene quickly when conflict occurs. These processes work well for the vast majority of students in schools. The presence of a restorative culture in the school and restorative practices in classrooms can also reassure students that they are safe and will be dealt with fairly when conflict does occur. Establishing mentoring and antibullying programs in schools will further enhance students' sense of security and reduce risk of serious incidents occurring that can escalate further into ongoing conflict and rifts among students. Strong home-school relationships will also enhance the capacity of the school to be culturally responsive to all its students and to the school community generally.

4 A Framework for Child-Focused Interventions

S choolwide behavior expectations and the principles of restorative practices described in Chapter 3 address the kinds of minor behavior challenges or first offenses typical of students in the general school population and at various times for individual children. This chapter focuses on interventions for students whose behavioral challenges are more severe and/or persistent, thus requiring structured and individualized planning to enable them to learn and to ensure their own and others' safety. Classroom teachers may need access to specialist advice to help them implement secondary interventions for as many as 15% of their students who present social, emotional, and behavioral challenges at various times during the school year. Another 3% to 5% of the school population exhibit ongoing and more severe behavioral difficulties requiring specialist consultation to design tertiary intervention programs that may also entail supplemental services outside school. This chapter highlights the principal's role in supporting these specialized interventions and provides an overview of the four-component intervention model for children whose challenging behaviors require individualized support.

ETHICAL AND LEGAL ISSUES

In their practice, school leaders continuously accommodate ethical guidelines and requirements in their interactions with students, their families, staff members, and the surrounding school community. There are also legal requirements and issues affecting school policy, and school leaders need information about student and family eligibility for and availability of support and services in the region. Legislative requirements and litigative precedents can vary in different states and regions, and a detailed consideration of these issues is beyond the scope of this guide. Nevertheless, every school needs clear policy and guidelines for addressing crucial ethical and legal issues that are directly relevant to school disciplinary practices and how the school responds to behavioral challenges. These will include, for example:

1. *Confidentiality*: Confidentiality within the restorative group meetings is important; what are the problems when community leaders and elders are invited to conferences? Many indigenous groups do not view privacy in the same way that Westerners do; for example, they may consider that the problem belongs to a wider family grouping beyond the biological parents of the child. Limits to confidentiality when addressing student concerns are covered in Chapter 5.

2. *Issues of consent*: Which children have rights to make decisions and to not have parents involved? There will be legal requirements in your region, and there may also be district policy about consent for different issues. Informed consent by the student is also an important consideration, as ideally the student should be in agreement with the conditions of the intervention plan.

3. *Reporting requirements*: There are strict laws in the United States and other countries regarding reporting physical and/or sexual abuse. Mandatory reporting laws are in effect in all states—teachers and principals are obliged to report suspected cases of abuse. Teachers and principals can ask general questions to establish suspicion of abuse that triggers mandatory reporting, but there are well-established parameters around what can be asked and discussed of the child and others as part of the reporting process. School personnel may not carry out formal interviews to establish the presence of abuse; doing so without proper training can seriously interfere with and even undermine later formal proceedings. These interviews must be and will be done by trained *evidential interviewers* who work for child protective services or the police once a report is made.

4. *Case management responsibility*: If the student who exhibits challenging behavior is also receiving services from a mental health agency, who is really in charge of the case? Who decides about medications? What should be done for students who are emancipated minors and do not have any parent in authority over them?

5. *Substance abuse*: What requirements exist regarding drug offenses, and what is legal and what is not?

6. *Health issues*: What of teenage girls who are pregnant? Most school districts have a program to allow them to finish school or a policy that provides for them to continue to attend their community school.

7. *Local authorities*: The principal works under the authority of a superintendent and a school board. How much say do those authorities have to make decisions about adopting current ideas? In Section I, we described general processes for keeping the school board informed of new developments in the school, but you'll need to know parameters for adoption and adaptation decisions affecting school discipline. Private and/or religious (parochial) schools will also have overseeing bodies or decision makers who may determine directions and/or must be consulted. Some schools that are separate from state control may condone discipline practices that run counter to public school practices, such as using a more punishment-oriented approach and having a heavy focus on morals.

8. *Adjudication and criminal incarceration implications*: If a student is incarcerated because of a serious crime (e.g., placed in a detention home or a juvenile detention facility), has the school any responsibility to follow up and keep tabs on the student's educational progress? Do those students continue to belong to the school and is their *acceptance* complete or only partial?

9. *Weapons policies*: Some principals have to deal with weapons policies—carrying a knife or worse. Metal detectors are common in some schools and may be characteristic of all schools in an entire school district. What are the rights around search and seizure (drugs, weapons, cell phones, iPods, etc.)?

10. *Right to effective treatment*: School leaders will be held accountable for introducing evidence-based procedures, and Response to Intervention (RTI) in particular requires accountability that includes record keeping about individualized interventions and the monitoring of student progress with behavioral records. If you follow the procedures described in this guide (see Chapter 2), you'll have a record-keeping system that can easily be adapted to meet context-specific legal requirements.

11. *Statutory and litigative mandates*: Your school will be subject to particular state laws or even regional mandates that have emerged

following litigation or legal actions. In the State of Hawai'i, for example, the Felix consent decree (U.S. District Court, Honolulu, HI, October 25, 1994) imposed additional requirements for students receiving special education services beyond those specified in Individuals with Disabilities Education Improvement Act (IDEIA).

12. *Special education requirements*: The various mandatory requirements for referrals, services, and supports are likely to be well understood by school principals, and there will be policy and guidelines in your district regarding specific requirements in different circumstances, situations, and school settings. It may not be clear, however, whether or not the student's individualized educational program (IEP) should include behavioral goals. Your district or state may have specific policy and/or guidelines relevant to behavioral planning for individual students who have ongoing behavioral challenges.

SECONDARY AND TERTIARY PREVENTION AND INTERVENTION

In 1996, Walker and his colleagues published their description of the three-level approach to organizing intervention supports and services for students with emotional and behavioral disorders, which has been widely adopted across the United States. According to this model, specific prevention or intervention approaches are tailored to the three levels—primary (Level 1), secondary (Level 2), and tertiary (Level 3). The cascade model of services for special education articulated many years ago by Deno (1970) utilized a pyramid to illustrate roughly the different percentages of children who would need different levels of support and services, starting from the broad base of regular education to the point of the pyramid with services for those requiring the most intensive support. According to the three-level approach, primary or Level 1 supports parallel the broad base in referring to the majority of children in school who respond positively to what Walker et al. (1996) termed "universal interventions"—schoolwide discipline guidelines, instruction in selected interpersonal skills (e.g., conflict resolution), and effective teaching and schooling. All children are seen as entering school ready and eager to learn: They generally pay attention, listen to teacher instructions, interact positively with classmates, engage in learning activities, and do their best on classroom assignments, homework, and assessments. These children do not require ongoing services other than occasional reminders as they can also make mistakes, get frustrated, overreact, bring problems from home to school, and sometimes get into or cause trouble for teachers and peers. Generally, however, their difficulties are short lived and respond well to ongoing evidence-based regular education practices in schools and classrooms.

Fuchs, Fuchs, and Stecker (2010) note that IDEIA as a special education entitlement builds on the expectation that schools already have in place empirically based Level 1 schoolwide programs. Appropriate use of special education services relies on a solid foundation of regular education with ongoing activities to ensure that grade-level curricula and pedagogies are research-based practices that have been shown to be effective in promoting positive learning and behavior for the majority of children. Among these are evidence-based pedagogical practices such as cooperative learning, direct instruction, and peer tutoring. Similarly, we describe strategies and systems for schoolwide discipline (see especially Chapters 1, 2, and 4) that also represent Level 1 approaches demonstrated to be effective for managing the behavior of the majority of students who only rarely break school rules. The percentage of students whose needs will be met by these primary Level 1 approaches is generally accepted to be approximately 80% to 85% (Curwin & Mendler, 1999; Wanzek & Vaughn, 2009).

Secondary and tertiary level services are for those students whose needs go beyond regular education services. Secondary prevention or Level 2 refers to the approximately 15% of children in school who will periodically require additional specialized services and support such as small group or embedded tutoring services. This percentage of the school population includes high incidence diagnoses such as learning disabilities and mild to moderate behavioral disorders. Burns and Gibbons (2008) describe how the RTI model enhances services to children and makes special education services available to children early rather than waiting for them to fail. Level 2 services may involve individualized in-class tutoring, resource room instruction, and in some cases part- to full-time placements in self-contained classrooms. Much of the discussion and debate around the effectiveness of the RTI policy involves the extent to which early response to identified educational needs can prevent placement in more stigmatizing placements requiring diagnostic labels. There is an expectation that Level 2 services are not permanent for individual children, but represent additional support required for different time periods and across school years—though IDEIA requires periodic evaluation to make these decisions.

Finally, some children and youth in school exhibit learning and behavioral needs that require intensive tertiary prevention and Level 3 support for extended periods of time, perhaps all through the school years. Children requiring Level 3 interventions may exhibit chronic, severe, and ongoing behavioral challenges and have been diagnosed as having a conduct disorder, developmental disability, and/or emotional disorder requiring longer-term individualized interventions. They may have dual diagnoses such as autism and developmental disabilities or oppositional defiant disorder and severe learning disabilities. Fuchs et al. (2010) report that up to 5% of school-age students in the United States prove to be unresponsive to secondary or Level 2 interventions, requiring more intensive intervention at Level 3.

Regular education was originally designed for the majority of children who respond well to primary prevention approaches. As a system, regular education has done less well with children who require secondary prevention supports and has not typically included those who require tertiary or Level 3 interventions. Historically, special education was designed primarily to address secondary and tertiary support needs, but it too has performed least well with students exhibiting severe behaviors. This chapter deals with all children who evidence difficulty following the school's behavioral expectations, ranging from those who only occasionally require support to those whose problem behaviors are severe and ongoing. This chapter and Chapters 5 and 6 focus on behaviors that are disruptive, stressful, and may even raise safety concerns for classmates, the teacher, and the students themselves. One approach that schools have used has been the adoption of zero-tolerance policies designed to reduce violence and behavior problems in schools. This hasn't worked, and a review of 10 years of research reports that zero-tolerance practices have actually been associated with increases in challenging behavior as well as school drop-out prior to graduation (American Psychological Association Zero Tolerance Task Force, 2006). Greene (2008) explains that zero-tolerance punitive responses to behaviors are not effective with children who have social, emotional, and behavior challenges because they typically do not have the skills to behave differently. In contrast, these handbooks integrate evidence-based school and classroomwide systemic approache with individualized intervention approaches across all levels of need.

Intervention: Level 2 and 3 Child-Focused Planning and Intervention

Schoolwide restorative practices support positive school and classroom climates wherein the majority of students receive the support necessary to achieve and to develop socioemotionally. This section addresses the school leader's role in supporting Level 2 and Level 3 interventions designed for individual children who are not responding to best practice in regular classrooms without additional services.

Deficit Discussions About Children

School leaders can have a major impact on how the school community thinks about students who exhibit challenging behavior. Rather than emphasizing student deficits and shortcomings, school leaders need to encourage a strengths-based approach to planning and problem solving when dealing with challenging behaviors. All students have support needs and are in the process of acquiring the multitude of understandings, competencies, and skills to become productive, prosocial adults who make valued contributions to their communities. Children who display chronic challenging behavior also have strengths, which are increasingly overshadowed by negative factors as the year progresses and they gain a reputation in the school. Children may even start the school year with their bad behavior from the previous year following them relentlessly so that they don't really have a chance to start fresh with a new teacher who isn't immediately on guard—waiting for the student to put a foot wrong. When a student has a reputation for being a problem at school, this also puts school personnel at risk for blaming those problems on *deficits within the child*. It becomes tempting to engage in deficit thinking that lures staff into denying agency for making a difference in the life of that child or young person.

Greene (2008) has written a powerful book about children who are *lost at school*. He urges all of us to take a long hard look at conversations about children that actually reveal negative attitudes and interpretations going far beyond behavioral evidence. Table 4 can be used to stimulate discussion about the kinds of negative comments that can undermine restorative approaches with individual children. Staff could be challenged to brainstorm respectful but constructively critical responses to different examples of deficit thinking in future conversations.

Interagency Services and Referrals

One issue for the school principal will be the appropriateness of referral to, for example, mental health agencies for additional child and family support. In most parts of the United States, there are now also formal requirements for documenting that the school has tried available best practices. Yet, schools can overrefer and thus pathologize what might be fairly typical problems, particularly during the adolescent years. On the other hand, appropriate questions need to be asked as to whether the behavioral challenges of a student meet criteria for an established psychiatric disorder. Depression, for instance, may well be disguised as angry interactions with teachers and peers, and anxiety may be the reason for a student avoiding activities, thus being noncompliant.

Table 4   Rethinking Negative Conversations About Children With Challenging Behavior

Comment	Questions	Possible Responses
He does that to get attention.	But isn't it okay for a child to want attention? Is he getting attention when he is doing something positive? Doesn't the child know what to do to get attention in positive ways?	
She wants things her way.	Don't we all want things our way at least some of the time? Does the child know how to negotiate getting what he wants some of the time?	
He's being manipulative.	Does this child really have the skills to be manipulative intentionally? If he is pushing my buttons, is this really his fault or is it because I'm not controlling my behavior as the adult?	
She just doesn't care about learning/ school.	Would she have any good reason to care—is school a positive place for her? Is she having any success at all in learning, or is school mostly punishing for her?	
He makes bad choices.	Is it possible that the bad choice he makes ends up getting him what he wants? Would an alternative good choice lead to a positive outcome for him? Does he have the skills to make other choices?	
She comes from a bad home.	Why is this relevant to her relationships and behavior in school? What do we really know about her home anyway? And even if the home is dysfunctional, why can't school be a positive experience for her?	
He's naughty.	Maybe, but when our own children are naughty, don't we intervene? What are we doing to make "being naughty" functional for him? Is he naughty all the time, or only in certain circumstances, certain places, and with certain people? Why?	

Comment	Questions	Possible Responses
She behaves that way because she's mentally ill, because she has ADHD, etc.	Does repeating the child's disability label really explain this particular incident? How can we build on her strengths rather than emphasize what's wrong?	
His older brother was exactly the same/just as bad.	Is it possible that the whole family is stigmatized at this school—so this child doesn't have a chance to do well? Is the older brother's behavior relevant to what to do with this child? If we weren't successful in turning around the older brother, can we do a better job with this child?	

Source: Adapted from a discussion in Greene (2008, pp. 12–13).

A student who exhibits serious behaviors may already have a history of challenging behavior. Where this is so, it is likely that other agencies in addition to the school will be involved with the child and his or her family. Common examples are mental health agencies, social welfare agencies (including child protection services), and the juvenile justice system (including family court, the police, and youth detention facilities). There is often confusion of responsibility when more than one public agency is involved with a young person. For example, a teenager with autistic spectrum disorder who is in the care of a foster family and has a significant health concern such as asthma or a seizure disorder is likely to have needs across a wide range of professional services as well as public and private community agencies. Some of these agencies may well have a case manager who is able to coordinate services, and sometimes a school psychologist or counselor might take on this role. Frequently, however, it will be up to the school principal to ensure that effective communication and joint decision making occurs across all the relevant services.

Principals may also be concerned about whether the school has adequate documentation to support a student referral to special education and whether the necessary financial resources will be available even if they make the referral. This can be the result of school budget cuts and increased pressure on public financing, federal assistance, and so on. Schools are being challenged to think practically and economically about the costs of programs and where alternative resources can be found. One such alternative is to link with easily accessed websites, such as the

School Mental Health Project at the University of California, Los Angeles (see smhp.psych.ucla.edu), for valuable evidence-based resources that are free. This chapter does not include descriptions of requirements for referrals to and the provision of special education and support services to children with disabilities, including emotional and behavioral disorders. Principals already have access to and knowledge about well-specified procedures and legal requirements (see, for example, Rosen, 2005). What is crucial is that the principal is willing to take on a leadership role in ensuring that cooperation and collaboration are strong across all relevant local agencies.

Implementing Interventions for Individual Children

There will be some children at school whose behavioral needs do require structured interventions, sometimes for periods of time and even indefinitely. Children who present ongoing challenges to school rules and for even the best teachers are likely to be diagnosed with labels such as *severe conduct disorders, anxiety disorders, attention deficit/hyperactivity disorder (ADHD), autism,* and *severe/profound developmental disabilities* with challenging behavior such as self-injury. Intensive individualized interventions should be provided for these children, whereby specialist personnel (e.g., the school psychologist or special education professional) work closely with school personnel, including the child's teacher and others with whom the child interacts, to design and implement effective intervention strategies that will enable the child to be successful at school. The next section of this chapter provides an overview of comprehensive four-component interventions that have been supported by research as effective in regular school settings accompanied by specialist support for the school, the child, and his or her family.

Four-component interventions

There are four specific components necessary for secondary and tertiary level interventions:

1. *Prevent*: Establish positive environments and social relationships that are culturally safe with clear expectations and supports for positive discipline.

2. *Educate*: Teach replacement skills that are appropriate behaviors to replace challenging behavior and that have higher functional utility in the classroom, school, and community compared with the original behavior problem.

3. *Restore*: Ensure that consequences for behavior are natural, including both positive and negative consequences that provide the student and others involved with the opportunity to restore relationships and preserve individual dignity and mutual respect.

4. *Think*: Examine the underlying understandings, interpretations, and emotions surrounding behavioral expectations, events, and incidents held by the student as well as by mediators—teachers, peers, family members, and others who interact with the young person.

The next sections explain why each of the four components is an important part of an effective intervention plan. Details about specific procedures to design and implement these four components are found in *The Teacher's Guide* and *The Consultant's Guide*.

Prevent—Antecedent settings and events

This principle is based on the obvious fact that no child misbehaves all of the time and across all contexts or situations. We need to understand the sorts of situations that trigger challenging behavior. These can be physical triggers, particularly for children with significant disabilities, such as a child with autism reacting negatively to loud noises, foods to which he or she is allergic, or confusing situations that overload the child's sensory system. More often than not, however, the triggers are social and interpersonal, such as when a student suddenly snaps and responds violently to an insult or taunt. Sometimes these situational variables are not the immediate ones in which the student reacts but set the stage for a negative emotional reaction, such as having a fight with parents before coming to school or witnessing domestic violence between parents. Antecedent events that happened outside school and/or in the past are likely not known to the school yet can be responsible for extreme tension, anxiety, and depression in a student who is then much less able to handle the ordinary everyday events that might cause a calmer student nothing more than minor annoyance. In addition, remember that environments can facilitate negative behavior by what they do *not* elicit or trigger. When educational environments are poorly structured, boring (fail to engage young minds in interesting activities), or resource limited (what are sometimes called *deficit environments*), positive behaviors are less likely, and negative behaviors occur in their place.

Greene (2008) asserts that "Most kids with behavioral challenges have five or six unresolved problems that are routinely precipitating their challenging episodes" (p. 75). He recommends that these precipitating problems should be resolved one by one so that in the future they are no longer leading to challenging episodes. The procedures you have put into place in your school to report incidents will help you to identify precipitating events or the kinds of situations and interactions that typically lead to a serious behavior for the child. But it is highly likely that such events, situations, and interactions can be permanently prevented from ever occurring in different environments and at future times for a child. This means that until the child acquires the skills and understandings needed to respond more adaptively to antecedents that are problematic, that student is at risk for continuing to display challenging behavior.

Thus, an important component of any intervention plan is *ecological*— to *prevent* precipitating events and circumstances from happening by rearranging the most predictable environmental triggers. Behavioral psychologists describe these as the *antecedents* of a behavior, acknowledging that some antecedents will be immediately identifiable to the watchful eye whereas others may be things that happened to the child when you were not watching. In the early stages of an intervention, avoiding difficult antecedent events and negative situations altogether may be crucial because the student hasn't yet learned either the skills or cognitive controls to prevent negative behavior reactions that have become ingrained habits. In the early stages of acquiring new skills to react differently, it will be easier and even tempting for the student to fall back on old habits. Gradually, the student can be exposed to risky situations in a way that enables practice of new skills and developing fluency in responding with those new skills— rather than with challenging behavior.

Ultimately, negative events associated with challenging behavior cannot be prevented from happening. The goal, however, is to try to at least prevent those that are most negative from occurring while the educative components of the intervention plan are being mastered. The student needs to acquire new, adaptive skills and understandings to respond to the inevitable ups and downs of real life. An analogy might be putting restrictions on the amount and kinds of food you have in the house during the early stages of weight loss—once better eating habits have been developed, one can eat just a few chips and then stop rather than eating the entire bag at once. Thus, a student described as having poor frustration tolerance may not be able to handle a worksheet with 25 mathematics problems, but the student might be able to tolerate working on the same number of problems if presented fewer at a time on different worksheets— provided he or she knew that there was an end in sight! Anger management provides another example: Whereas one person responds to provocation calmly and logically, another person may lash out physically and cause harm. Anger management programs work by teaching new anger control skills that are practiced with the gradual introduction of exposure to the kinds of risky situations that used to result in loss of control. Children with social, emotional, and behavior challenges in the early stages of an intervention plan should receive additional support from adults and peers who can prevent and mediate conflict and confrontations that they cannot handle. Seating arrangements, for example, may be crucial in the early stages of an anger management program to ensure that a student is not in proximity to other students associated with past conflict, whereas at a later stage in an intervention program the student will have acquired skills to prevent conflict.

Educate—Teaching positive replacement skills

This principle is based on the presumption that all behavior serves some sort of function—even socially undesirable and inappropriate actions by students often work for them. If one ever hopes to discourage these behaviors, the young person needs to have acceptable alternative behaviors and skills that will offer equivalent levels of rewarding outcomes. If we can figure out what functions the behavior serves or the benefits that the student receives, then we can try to encourage replacement skills that will work just as well but be socially acceptable or less harmful to all concerned.

Old fashioned and outdated behavior management practices were based almost exclusively on the sole application of the principles of contingency management: reinforcement and punishment. Good behavior was to be rewarded, which in turn would lead to increases in that behavior. Undesired behavior should not be rewarded (but instead extinguished through punishment or planned ignoring), which would result in a decrease in the behavior. Unfortunately, this simple formula doesn't explain what to do when the child doesn't have the skills to use a positive behavior (e.g., negotiation) but does have skills in negative behavior (e.g., fighting) that gets the desired results (i.e., the reward) for the child at least some of the time. The missing step in the process is identifying the skills that the child needs to learn and then learn to use to replace challenging behavior. Sometimes, the needed replacement or positive alternative skill is specific to a particular problem (such as negotiating instead of fighting or a social skill that facilitates group interaction instead of being domineering). But often, the replacement skills required are rather general—applicable to a range of situations and needs. An important example of a general skill is that of self-control, now widely recognized as an ability that is essential for managing negative feelings like anger or social situations like waiting one's turn.

Information about the sequence of events associated with a child's negative behavior will provide valuable clues about the purpose or function of the behavior. For example, if a student is continuously referred to the office by one or more teachers for disruptive behavior in the classroom, it is important to know much more about what happened in order to not simply punish the student but prevent similar incidents from happening in the future. Without identifying the harm that was done and using restorative practices to make amends, the student is not given the opportunity nor expected to make things right but instead is actually encouraged to continue to be disruptive lest he lose face in front of others. Table 5 presents a typical scenario likely to lead to an office referral for a student named Samuel in middle school. The scenario illustrates how everyone in the room becomes locked into a negative interaction pattern that almost seems to require escalation rather than starting anew. As you review the scenario, keep in mind that both the teacher and classmates could have chosen to engage in different, replacement behaviors that might have affected Samuel's behavior differently as well. But a crucial point to review is whether or not Samuel actually has the skills needed to behave any differently than he did. What do you think?

Table 5   Samuel's Challenge in Math Class

Review the following sequence of events in a math class that ended with Samuel being referred to the office. For each step in the sequence, identify a possible alternative skill scenario that might have occurred and could have replaced the negative antecedents and behaviors that actually happened.

What Happened	Possible Alternative Skill Scenario
The teacher tells students to review briefly the pages assigned as math homework the night before and independently complete a worksheet she has handed out to assess their understanding.	
Samuel didn't read the pages in the textbook assigned by the teacher the night before, and he also doesn't have a pencil with him.	
Samuel raises his hand and loudly asks the teacher for a pencil, which she gives him while commenting that this is the fifth pencil she has given him that month.	
Samuel doesn't know any of the answers so starts to draw graffiti-type scribbles on his worksheet	
Students seated on either side of Samuel start to laugh, and Samuel says loudly, "What are you laughing at, you #@*%&er!"	

What Happened	Possible Alternative Skill Scenario
The teacher looks up and says, "Samuel, quiet!"	
Samuel growls but starts drawing again, pushing hard on the pencil so that the lead breaks.	
Samuel gets out of his seat and walks to the pencil sharpener where he makes quite a show of things, then taps several desks with the tip of his pencil while walking back to his seat.	
A student mutters "Stop that, you jerk!" in a low voice that the teacher doesn't hear.	
Samuel says loudly, "Why should I, loser!"	
The teacher hears this and says loudly, "Samuel, don't make me have to tell you again!"	
Samuel smiles defiantly and says, "Or you'll do what to me?"	

A negative pattern between the teacher and a student such as this one can become so entrenched that being sent to the office, which is intended to be punishment, becomes reinforcement for both the teacher and the student. The teacher could be forgiven for thinking that the rest of the class period will go better once Samuel leaves the room. And Samuel may consider it worth it to avoid doing the math worksheet and having to reveal to everyone that he cannot in fact answer the questions. Worse, in the long run, the only way to prevent future occurrences of the behavior pattern above may be seen by all as achieved only by excluding Samuel from the class altogether.

Restore—Consequences not retribution

This principle is based on the simple fact that people do respond to reinforcement and that the possibility of gaining rewards is a powerful motivator of all human behavior. Interestingly, young people who have significant problem behaviors are often what psychologists call "reward dominant." That is to say they are more intent on gaining rewards than they are on avoiding punishment; sometimes, they may even seem immune to punishment, so caregivers keep increasing the intensity of punishments, which only makes matters worse as the child becomes increasingly resentful and angry. Many traditional approaches to discipline are really based on increasingly aversive consequences for undesirable behavior, when in fact punitive retribution often has little impact on the most challenging students. Harsh punishments, however justly deserved someone in authority might feel them to be, may not cause a reduction in the punished behavior but do cause resentment and feelings of hostility and antagonism to authority figures. Restorative justice practices focus much more on removing feelings of unfairness and finding rewards for improved behavior rather than punishments for past offenses.

Restorative school discipline does not mean that there will be no consequences for behavior. There will be natural consequences for negative behavior, and part of the purpose of schooling is to educate young people about expectations for their behavior as well as what will happen when they fail to meet those expectations. However natural and logical those consequences for negative behavior might be, consequences that do no more than punish the offender accomplish little or nothing toward fixing damage or harm that may have resulted from the behavioral incident. Consequences such as suspension and exclusion may have the desirable side effect of temporarily separating offenders from victims but, again, this is only a temporary solution unless amends are made to the satisfaction of all parties. Theoretically, suspension and removal from a negative situation provide participants opportunity to reflect on events, away from provocation or negative feelings. On the other hand, removal from the situation can also operate as reinforcement as the problem temporarily goes away; meanwhile, negative attributions may actually escalate as each participant nurtures hostile interpretations of events rather than exploring alternative interpretations that could heal relationships. Finally, punishment alone that is for the sole purpose of retribution is sometimes more applicable in the criminal justice system than it is for use in an educational context. The major purpose of an educational system and of schools is to educate young people to become productive citizens: schools should attempt to be beacons of enlightenment and remain true to their educational purpose.

This third component of effective interventions, therefore, is to ensure that consequences for behavior are restorative in supporting or providing opportunities for the restoration of relationships through mutual respect and the preservation of individual dignity and feelings that one's worth is recognized. When asked to explain disruptive behavior, school leaders are often likely to attribute it to the young person having "low self-esteem." But often the exact opposite is the case: The student has too positive a sense of self that is not reflected in his or her level of accomplishment. However, the facility with which some students claim they have been disrespected ("dissed") reveals the fundamental human need for some level of respect as a worthwhile individual.

Offenders and victims alike have the right to have their voices heard, and it is important that they hear one another's perceptions of events toward understanding what is needed to make amends and move forward. Review the scenario for Samuel in Table 5. Even where there isn't really a victim, as in this instance, a great deal can be done toward restoration of what appear to be damaged relationships between Samuel and his peers and between him and the teacher. Describe a mediation process—it could be shuttle mediation—that could be used to restore these relationships rather than punishments that might in fact increase Samuel's hostility toward the teacher and some of his classmates. Any consequences that are delivered to Samuel for his behavior must be consistent with what would happen for anyone else, but until Samuel has the necessary skills to stop a negative chain such as this from occurring, it will be up to the teacher and other school personnel to do so.

In any school, there needs to be agreement and consistency regarding the consequences for negative behavior. For example, where school expectations include coming to class with needed materials including pencils and textbooks, having a range of possible consequences that are applied idiosyncratically by different teachers with different students at different times can be problematic. Suppose the teacher delivers a gentle verbal reminder to Melissa for forgetting her pencil on Monday and on Tuesday reprimands Samuel sternly in a negative tone of voice for the same problem. Students will perceive differential treatment, and Samuel in particular will feel that he has been treated unfairly. We have seen school lists of a wide range of possible consequences for bringing cell phones to class, ranging from a temporary confiscation of the item to returning the item at the end of the semester or not at all, without any specificity regarding which of these will apply in any given instance. This creates huge potential for feelings of discrimination and favoritism as well as perceptions of being treated unfairly based on whether or not a particular teacher has it in for particular students. Particularly as this is the kind of violation that can be predicted and is likely to occur, it should be easy to reach consensus across school personnel about consistent, transparent, and fair application of consequences for transgressions—not leave this to the moment. Moment-to-moment decisions about consequences for misbehavior run the risk of being fueled by the adult's annoyance or anger at that moment of time. When teachers feel threatened, provoked, frustrated, or made to feel anxious, their negative emotional responses will often cause them to overreact. That is perfectly normal human behavior, but it is very helpful for teachers to have clearly established rules for ensuring that the consequences fit the crime.

Where transgressions are serious and actual harm has occurred or been threatened, the important need to redress that harm should be done in a way that does not strip people of their dignity. If children are demeaned and/or feel humiliated during the process of trying to fix things, future recovery may become impossible. Children who are backed into a corner will save face by becoming more and more aggressive rather than lose what they see as the only remaining power they can exercise—defiance. By the time violence has occurred, responding in kind will only aggravate and increase hostilities for everyone. At that point, safety for everyone must be paramount, but attaining this does not have to be at the expense of relationships in the long run. The process for a formal restorative conference provides a structure to respond to serious behavior that has harmed or threatened to harm others, and in-school suspension provides a safe environment for the healing process to begin consistent with restorative school discipline (see Chapter 6).

Think—Teaching new understandings and thinking skills

This principle is based on the fact that undesirable challenging behavior is not just caused by past consequences but usually reflects some sort of motivational needs in the students or incorrect set of beliefs and understandings about the world. In most cultures, people have a need to feel valued and accepted, to feel important, to feel in control, and to feel some degree of autonomy over their own personal areas of responsibility. But young people can easily misjudge situations. For example, one reason young people might give in to peer pressure is because they fear rejection, even though they might recognize the actions that are being encouraged by their peers are silly, dangerous, or irresponsible. So we need to try to understand young people's motives, their judgments, and their understandings and beliefs.

In addition to learning new skills and practicing positive adaptive behaviors, students with challenging behavior are likely to have distorted underlying understandings, interpretations, and emotions about events, circumstances, and even their relationships with other people. Greene (2008) emphasizes that children with challenging behavior and with social and emotional problems lack "important thinking skills" (p. 10). In association with ongoing conflict at home and in school, there may also be some truth to perceptions of rejection and hostility from others—teachers, peers, family members, and others who interact with the young person. Inevitably, teachers serve as caregivers who may feel they are treated badly by the child in response to genuine attempts to help and offer support. This may lead to exaggerated responses to challenging behavior, which in turn results in even more negative behavior from the student. This ugly cycle escalates to the point that the teacher may struggle with being able to act as a positive mediator in carrying out intervention plans. The next section discusses the issue of mediators and how to strengthen their role in positive ways. Here, however, it is important to acknowledge that negative interaction patterns are likely to have become established in interactions with others at school and that the child perceives that others don't care, dislike him or her, or are even "out to get me."

Contemporary cognitive behavioral approaches to interventions address not only the observable skills and behaviors that become new actions but also the thinking behind events and behavior. Young people diagnosed as having severe conduct disorders may not only demonstrate negative acting out behavior that is harmful to others, but they may also misjudge the actions of others. Psychologists have shown that aggressive children often misjudge the intent of other students—they tend to see their peers as having hostile intentions, and that causes them to respond with hostile aggression (Dodge, 1980). Interpretations of hostile intent mean that a perfectly innocent mistake such as bumping into someone in the school corridor will be interpreted as a deliberate act intended to cause harm, embarrassment, or disrespect. Children who ascribe hostile intent to the acts of others as almost their default interpretation require interventions that focus on both new skills and understandings about behavior—how they think about events and circumstances.

There are also some children who will be diagnosed as having severe conduct disorders who appear to lack the capacity for empathy and seem unable to see situations from another point of view. Some of these students show callous disregard for others and require specialized, personal intervention or therapy, precluding the opportunity to cause further harm to their victims. The number of such children will be very small, but it would be a mistake to assume that every child has a well-developed sense of empathy and does not deliberately intend to cause harm to someone else. These students require intervention so that they learn to be reflective and appreciate the impact of their actions on others. For them, the *think* component of four-part interventions is crucial; without this component, none of the other three could have an impact until these dysfunctional cognitions and intentions are altered.

CULTURALLY RESPONSIVE RESTORATIVE PRACTICES

Think for a moment about how, in your own family of origin, and in your current family experience, you try to resolve conflict and how you try, after some kind of altercation, to get everyone in the family back to an even keel and to move on in a more harmonious way, without recriminations or ongoing retaliation. There are probably hundreds of different ways whereby couples kiss and make up, and families seek some sort of cathartic outpouring of emotion and criticism, followed by healing expressions of regret, apology, and forgiveness. Cultures and generations that are not particularly prone to vent their feelings might be more prone to use silence, hurt, and avoidance until the incident is forgotten and emotions have dissipated. Other cultures, more emotionally volatile, might be quite used to having a ding-dong battle with yelling and throwing objects until everyone is too exhausted to care anymore. Hollywood movies and TV shows are full of examples of these kinds of typical family conflicts and atypical ways of dealing with them! The point is that there are huge individual differences, across and within cultures, across the generations, within different religions, and between genders.

Restorative justice as a principle had its origins in the way some Native American and other indigenous cultures traditionally approached social crimes and punishments. It was actually the attempt by colonial societies to recognize that indigenous peoples had alternative systems that led to the greater support for restorative justice in countries such as Australia, New Zealand, Canada, Scotland, and the United States. Traditional patterns of everyone in the involved community getting together and talking openly and honestly about feelings and seeking consensual solutions allowed restorative justice ideas to be extended to cultures that do not traditionally focus so strongly on the processes of finding a common, healing solution. Because of this, we recognize that restorative justice approaches as used in a school will seem quite foreign to some individuals and will seem absolutely natural to others. Thus, school leaders are faced with something of a challenge when introducing this approach to diverse parent, family, and community groups.

In order to accommodate such diversity, the trick is to focus very clearly on the values and ideas behind the approach and not to try to follow any particular process or method in a formulaic fashion. Find out what the individuals concerned feel comfortable with. This is particularly crucial if the parties to the problem themselves come from different cultural perspectives. A family that is used to spending long periods of time talking an issue out will not gel very well with a family that prefers to push problems under the rug and move on. Teachers who believe very strongly in personal responsibility will not find it easy to engage in a discussion in which the behavior of concern is being understood in a psychological and social context—such teachers will see it as a soft option, molly-coddling students, and trying to excuse totally inexcusable behavior. They might agree with, for example, resistance to the idea of restorative justice in French society, which celebrates its highly codified legal system. Other teachers may feel that the approach fails to give proper respect to victims' voices and rights and the role of the school in upholding them.

Focusing on the principles can be achieved by encouraging reluctant or hesitant participants to think of a time when they have made a mistake, performed a transgression, or done something hurtful that they now regret. How would they want to be treated by the offended party? How would they best be able to make amends? What in their experience would allow some sort of healing to occur? In answering the questions, individuals will reveal their own often deep-seated cultural and religious beliefs about the fundamental principles of justice: acknowledgment, apology, forgiveness, accepting natural consequences, making amends, understanding who has been harmed or affected (beyond the obvious victim), and rallying social support to the perpetrator's genuine efforts to improve.

The accepted way of achieving these principles might be quite varied across cultures, but the principles themselves seem to be rather similar. Try to focus on the principles and not on the method. For example, African Americans and young people from Pacific nations such as Fiji will, as a mark of respect, tend to lower their eyes and be silent when addressed by older individuals with greater social standing. One could not expect a young person from such cultures to engage actively in a group discussion. In New Zealand, processes conducted by elders on the *marae* (the traditional meeting house) have achieving community peace as a primary goal, with less of a focus on the victim's interests. When discussing cultural differences, however, the greatest danger is overgeneralization: young people from a given ethnic group do not necessarily identify with that culture or know anything at all about its traditions. Instead, they may identify far more with what can be referred to as "teenage culture," to give one example. Peacemaking, dispute resolution, and rebuilding relationships are what we need to focus on. The method for achieving positive outcomes can vary according to your best judgment of the predilections and expectations of the individual students, teachers, and families involved.

THE ROLE OF MEDIATORS IN INTERVENTIONS

An important focus of this chapter is the role played by *mediators*: All behavioral intervention programs are put into place—whether directly (and planfully) or indirectly (naturalistically)—by persons who have a relationship with and some degree of influence on the young person of concern. These significant others are mediators in that they have a mediating effect on the student—now and in the future—and how they carry out this mediating role can in turn make the difference between a successful or unsuccessful intervention program.

The published literature on intervening with behavior challenges has tended to emphasize training for mediators to ensure that they have the skills and understandings needed to be effective as intervention agents. While these skills are important, an exclusive focus on skill building runs the risk of neglecting the need to attend to the relationship between the child and the adult mediator. By the time a student is referred for formal intervention of some kind, it is likely that the student's relationships with others have also been affected—sometimes quite negatively. It may even be that a teacher actually has grown to dislike the student or may avoid interactions altogether with that student rather than experience negative feelings. It is unfortunate that the literature is silent on this issue, as the child needs to feel cared for and valued to be motivated to change to the new behaviors that those adults expect: Children know when they are not liked, even when adults have convinced themselves and others that they are showing no visible signs of rejection. Thus, we advocate a procedure called *positive affective priming* (Evans, 2010) as an important step in the intervention process, enabling the adult who interacts with the child to experience positive feelings that will then have a positive impact on future interactions.

Activity: Positive Affective Priming

Rationale: In cases where there has been conflict between the teacher and a student for whom a formal behavior intervention program is developed, the teacher may harbor negative attitudes toward that child. Unless acknowledged and addressed, these negative attitudes may later interfere with establishing the kinds of positive interpersonal interactions needed for the child's efforts to be rewarded by the teacher. The teacher needs to view the student in a different, more positive light.

What to do: The teacher might ask the student's mother and father if they would share some photographs of the student starting at a very young age and continuing until now. These photographs should be ones that the family and the student like a great deal, including photographs of the student smiling, playing a game that he or she enjoys, being positive, being nice to a younger sibling, and so on. If the parents are reluctant to loan the photos to the teacher to take home for 2 to 3 days, ask the parents if they would meet with you after school and look at the photos with you: This could actually be a very pleasant experience for the teacher and the family. If there is such a meeting with the family, remember that the purpose of the photo viewing is to see another side of the child, so this is not the time to talk about problems or revisit conflict. Keep the focus of the time together on positive stories about the pictures!

Follow-up: After viewing the photos, reflect on the student's good points and how nice he or she looked in so many of the pictures you saw. Think of new information and things you know about the student that you didn't know before. Does he or she have a pet you can ask about? What does he or she like to do with the family on weekends? Can you think of what nice things you might say to him or her even before class starts to set a positive tone on your relationship with this student?

Understanding the influences of mediators—teachers, friends, family—is a critical role for school leaders. For example, in most schools there is a dean, deputy principal, or other staff member who is designated as the individual who deals with discipline and punishment. It is important for school leaders to assess the way in which such a role is working. Does this role in any way undermine the authority, responsibility, and agency of teaching staff who may come to overrely on the enforcer? Similarly, a parent is a crucial mediator in the life of a child and can have an important influence: However, if we expect too much of parents in relationship to a teenage child, do we undermine and complicate further that parent's ability to support positive behavior change? And how might the normal teacher-student relationship be negatively affected if we fail to acknowledge what the teacher expects and needs as well as what the student expects and needs? Finally, friends can mediate whether or not an intervention will be successful or will fail—and the absence of even one positive (mediator) friend for support can make it doubly challenging to motivate a teenager to be part of the school community. Completing the Mediator Worksheet in Table 6 as a team can help develop appreciation of mediator perspectives on behavioral challenges relevant to intervention.

The Effort to Implement Scale in Table 7 is used by behavioral consultants to guide decision making about whether or not a particular intervention approach is likely to be doable for mediators. Teachers, for example, have multiple demands on their time and attention in the classroom, so knowing whether an intervention can fit within that context is important, or the intervention will not be implemented with integrity.

Table 6 The Mediator Worksheet

Target student:	Target mediators:
What do mediators want/need?	
What are mediators doing now and why are they doing this?	

(Continued)

(Continued)

How is it working to meet student's need for behavior change?
How is it working to meet mediator's needs now and in the future?
How can the intervention be changed to address both student's and mediators' needs?

Table 7 The Effort to Implement Scale

For each item below, rate the different aspects that require consideration if the intervention mediator is to implement the planned intervention, using the scale from 1 to 5, ranging from 1 as *low* effort to 5 as *high* effort based on your judgment regarding discrepancies between what now exists and what the intervention requires.

	Rating				
	Low		Average		High
1. Overall effort by the adult needed to implement the intervention	1	2	3	4	5
2. Resources needed (time and materials) to implement the intervention	1	2	3	4	5

	Rating		
	Low	Average	High
3. The cultural fit of the intervention	1 2	3 4	5
4. Technical skills needed to implement the intervention	1 2	3 4	5
5. The match between personal values and the intervention procedure for the person who will intervene	1 2	3 4	5
6. Perceptions by the interventionist that this plan is in the student's best interest	1 2	3 4	5

Source: Adapted from Schindler and Horner (2005).

SUMMARY

What do we mean by interventions that are *child focused*? We mean that when seriously challenging behavior occurs, we need to be very careful not to focus all our attention on the character of the young person who has exhibited the negative behavior. In psychology there is a well-known error of judgment called "the fundamental attribution error," which is to attribute behavior entirely to characteristics (usually negative) of the person rather than to see the behavior in context and to recognize that the situation plays a large role in regulating (causing) behavior. Perhaps we should have called this chapter "Child in Context Focused," but the general point is clear: we need to try to understand the student and his or her negative behavior before leaping into the task of consequating it.

Even the term *negative behavior*, of course, implies a judgment that can easily allow us to miss causal factors like ecological influences (triggers and setting events) or the student's lack of a more desirable alternative behavior. For these reasons, the term *challenging behavior* began to be introduced by consultants to remind us that the behavior challenges the system. Sometimes, it is the system or context that needs changing.

In a child-centered approach, we look at a model suggesting that when explaining challenging behavior there are typically a variety of causes. We have put these possible causes into four categories because we have found that in order to design an effective intervention, strategies designed to address all four categories of causal influence need to be considered. Any comprehensive treatment or intervention plan needs to consider environmental triggers and try to reduce the contexts that make the behavior more likely.

A fundamental part of the child-centered philosophy is to avoid stigmatizing the child who exhibits challenging behavior so that it becomes difficult for the teaching staff to come up with constructive interventions. One way to assist in countering such a trend is to consider strategies such as positive affective priming. Another strategy is inherent in the restorative justice model, which shifts the focus from blame and retribution to understanding and problem solving for the benefit of all. In that process, there is no need to follow a specific formula, such as having family group conferences or meetings between the victim and the perpetrator. The principles of restorative practices need to be interpreted according to cultural realities.

In mobilizing community support, cultures are respected and acknowledged. In addition to the role of volunteers serving on youth assistance panels, community support includes working closely with other agencies, particularly the juvenile justice system, which will inevitably be involved with the more serious behaviors. In the end, we can see that much of this discussion can be reframed as the importance of sustaining respectful relationships, even with the student who seems intent on making one's life as a principal quite miserable! The focus on positive relationships is not some Pollyanna-style mitigation of the serious consequences of severe behavior but, when accompanied by active, constructive, problem-focused interventions, actually ensures more successful outcomes, allowing the school to focus on its primary purpose: the development of students academically, socially, and emotionally.

5 Decisions About How the School Responds to Behavior

This chapter focuses on the role of the school leader in decisions about and procedures for school responses to student behavior. It introduces a way of thinking that distinguishes between behaviors that cause harm to others and behaviors that need attention but are not a direct threat to the safety of any other person. The school response to behavior must be consistent, fair, and transparent to staff and students so that the risk of arbitrary or overly punitive reactions is minimized and restorative practices can proceed without misunderstandings and misinterpretations. The chapter covers strategies for recording discipline incidents, emphasizing the importance of engaging the school community in distinguishing between major and minor behavior problems, particularly for behaviors considered to be harmful. Threat assessment is addressed, along with description of a process for the school to respond to threatening incidents systematically. Procedures described in the chapter provide the school leader with objective data at the time of the incidents as well as, over time, a running record for evaluation purposes.

MAKING DECISIONS ABOUT BEHAVIOR AND ITS CONSEQUENCES

An essential role for school leaders is to be able to judge the seriousness of behavioral incidents and to be able to estimate the riskiness of certain behaviors, what they signal, what the level of threat to safety might be, and how urgently behavior must be addressed (Skiba & Peterson, 2000). Seriousness is not meant to imply a level of punishment that is somehow appropriate for the seriousness of a behavior: this aspect is characteristic of a system of retribution where the punishment must fit the crime. In contrast, in a restorative discipline school, seriousness can be fundamental to identifying the degree of harm (or potential for harm) and thus the level of restoration that is needed in order to redress that harm—to make amends or restitution, not just to punish.

Not all behaviors require school interventions, though some of these may suggest appropriate referrals for nonschool services or advice for the child and family. Other behaviors should not be dismissed by schools even if they do not present a threat to others, such as the range of self-harm behaviors that need attention but are not a direct threat to the safety of any other person, such as cutting and other forms of self-injury. Still, other behaviors may put children at risk longer term, such as eating disorders and being overweight, which can contribute to behavioral difficulties. Obese children may be bullied, and eating disorders such as anorexia and bulimia can have serious health consequences for adolescents. There are other victimless behaviors such as being extremely socially isolated, and students who have no friends may be at risk for becoming victims or even aggressive victims who may in the future cause harm to others. There is also a range of inappropriate sexual behaviors that do not directly harm other students but which can become problematic and will be seen by the school community as particularly offensive: these include accessing pornography or voyeuristic behavior in the school's locker rooms and toilets. Finally, discipline policies are especially important for behavior problems that are not necessarily disruptive to school activities but which interfere considerably with successful learning: for example, smoking, drinking alcohol, and other drug use.

In most schools, the principal has access to the consultant services of a capable behavior specialist such as a school psychologist or counselor who can provide both ongoing and critical incident advice when needed. This consultant specialist should support the school in being engaged in the school's approach to restorative school discipline as well as provide services as part of intensive individualized interventions for eligible children (see the companion *Consultant's Guide* in this series). A consultant with specialist knowledge can support the school in the development of clear guidelines for determining which kinds of behaviors will be met with which kinds of consequences from the school. School psychologists and other behavior specialists will also have specific professional knowledge of risk assessment—recognizing what behaviors are likely to escalate into more serious difficulties.

School leaders are expected to respond effectively to behaviors that are or have the potential to be harmful to others, including students and staff. To meet such expectations without undermining restorative practices and a positive school climate, school leaders must ensure that their decisions reflect the seriousness of the incident and that those decisions and their consequences are clearly understood and accepted by the school community. Judgments about behavior and consequences that are left to the moment are highly likely to appear arbitrary—to both teachers and to students. Often, what can be interpreted as the very same behavior for two different children can actually result in a much more severe consequence for one student than for another student. School and district statistics on suspension, for example, reveal clear patterns of disproportionate ethnic representation. Even where teachers may be totally convinced that they are equitable about application of discipline operating with the same rules for all, students can often give examples of certain behavior by a favorite or white student being ignored, but the very same behavior by an African American resulting in a verbal reprimand.

Lack of transparency about discipline decisions arouses suspicions regarding equity and discrimination. Particularly for children who have ongoing behavioral challenges, lack of transparency about how the school responds to incidents will reinforce negative attributions and feelings of hostile intent. Interpretations of unfairness and discrimination are logical conclusions for children (and families) who feel they are always treated differently and unfairly in comparison to others who are favored or seen as having more power in the school community. Given that these are likely to be the students who are engaged in behavioral incidents most often, it is crucial that schools do not provide them with the opportunity to disengage at the onset of restorative processes by justifying feelings that they are once again being treated unfairly. Breaking this cycle is particularly important to build trust that supports new, positive behaviors and inclusion.

How can the school administration judge the seriousness of an offense? There are some simple principles that can be applied. For example, in a case of assault, what sort of weapons if any were used, what sorts of threats were made, was the violence triggered by anger or by fear, and has the behavior occurred before? In the analysis of criminal behavior, understanding what is called the "offense chain" is important. What sequence of events led up to the behavior? Was it planned or opportunistic? It is also important, when interviewing young people who have committed a serious transgression, to allow the interview to elicit the kinds of possibly distorted thinking that preceded the aggression. Good interview techniques by the principal, who will often be the individual asked to investigate an incident, can allow assessment of the degree to which the individual is remorseful, the degree to which he or she understands the seriousness of the offense, and whether he or she has empathy of any kind for the victim. Young people with psychopathic traits and who seem to have no empathy must be managed very differently from those who made a silly mistake and genuinely regret it. Note too that while restorative practices are under-way, there may also be natural consequences for some behavior such as aggression and criminal offenses. The difference is that punishment for the offense—retribution—is not allowed to become the only or even the most important outcome of a transgression; the desired outcome is doing what-ever is possible to make things right again and, if this is not possible, working toward ensuring no future repetitions of the behavior. These issues are closely related to the likelihood of success with a restorative practices approach (see Chapter 6).

Here is an example based on our recent experience. Shaun, a 14-year-old boy with Down syndrome, was on an overnight field trip with other youngsters in special education. At some point during the evening, he approached Melissa, a girl in the group also with Down syndrome, and said to her, "I'd like to feel your boobies," as he grabbed at her breasts. Melissa pulled away and walked off, and Shaun did nothing further. However, after getting home the next day, Melissa told her parents what had happened, and her parents called the police. The incident was now in the serious category because of the people involved, the legal aspects, the responsibilities of the teachers who had organized the field trip, and so on. How serious was the actual behavior? Obviously one cannot answer that question without much more information:

- Was this a first offense, or had Shaun shown sexualized behavior in the past?
- How much did Shaun understand about the importance of privacy and respect for one's own and others' bodies?
- When questioned, was Shaun able to explain why what he did was wrong and how it might have upset Melissa?
- What kinds of interactions had occurred between Shaun and Melissa *prior* to the incident? For example, had they been making consensual physical overtures, such as holding hands or kissing?
- Had Shaun ever been introduced to sex education?
- Did Shaun have more appropriate skills for approaching girls the way other typical teenagers might?
- What had Shaun's parents told him about sex?
- What did the incident reveal about Melissa's strategies and skills for dealing with (possibly unwanted) advances from boys?

- Were Melissa's parents somewhat overprotective, and why had they not contacted the school prior to involving the police in the incident?
- Was the field trip being properly supervised?
- As they are in the same class for the rest of the year, can a normal friendship between Melissa and Shaun be sustained?

Only when you have answers to all of these questions can the true seriousness of the behavior be judged, even though administratively the management of the incident is likely to be complicated. If the various parties involved have strong moral, religious, or other beliefs, or views about the degree to which people with intellectual disabilities can be held accountable for potentially illegal behavior, it is likely that any direct response to this behavior will be judged as too harsh or too lenient by someone. When the goal is restorative, however, the opinions of all relevant parties can be taken into consideration and a solution can be worked out to the satisfaction of everyone.

Schools with restorative practices will already have established fair and transparent rules for student conduct along with stated consequences for behavior outside the rules. Thus, schools that adopt a restorative practices culture have the foundation for behavior expectations that are both understood and considered to be fair across the school community (Chapter 1). Schoolwide Positive Behavior Support (SWPBS) is another approach that was designed to address comprehensively all behavioral challenges arising in a school, whether the student is part of the general education population or receiving special education services (see also www.pbis.org). SWPBS requires that schools specify objective, observable definitions of expectations for student behavior along with transparency about the kinds of consequences that will happen based on the nature and extent of particular behaviors (Sugai et al., 2005). For SWPBS to be effective, it must build on shared understandings about school behavioral expectations along with a set of processes and recording procedures to monitor both the student's behavior and what happens as a result of that behavior. This goes beyond stating positive examples of a school's behavioral expectations (Chapter 2) and requires careful delineation of acceptable and unacceptable behavior, along with decisions about whether an unacceptable behavior is minor or major. One risk with SWPBS, however, is that schools may see this system as another tool in the toolbox rather than as an overarching set of principles and practices as represented by restorative practices ingrained in the culture of the school.

Recording Behavioral Incidents Objectively

Several statistics provide evidence regarding behavioral challenges for schools. One such metric is the number and percentage of office discipline referrals (ODRs) filed by school personnel to record serious student behavior, which may or may not result in students being sent to the office but do result in a report or record of the incident (McIntosh, Campbell, Carter, & Zumbo, 2009). Some school systems also require and utilize formal student threat assessment reports that must be filed with the district (Strong & Cornell, 2008). These reporting devices may already be required by the school district but not necessarily used at the school as part of an ongoing process of restorative practices. The mechanisms described in the remainder of this chapter are designed in such a way that they can both fulfill district reporting requirements and be used at school level with teachers, students, and across the school community to reach better understandings about behavior consistent with the principles of restorative practices.

Office discipline referral

A system of ODRs is a formal process for recording, compiling, and analyzing incidents when student behavior failed to meet the behavior expectations established for the school. Virtually all schools will have such a system in place. There is value, however, in reviewing your system to ensure that it adheres to best practice as an objective process for identifying and recording problem behaviors and consequences to students when those behaviors occur. A good ODR serves several purposes simultaneously:

- Sufficient detail about incidents of problem behavior are reported using agreed definitions across the school; these are transparent to and understood by students, school personnel, and families.
- The requirement to file a formal incident record for minor and major behavior problems helps to protect personnel and students from charges of arbitrary application of discipline rules and consequence.
- The accumulation of ODRs for particular individual children may assist in identification of students who require additional services and supports.
- Regular monitoring of ODRs allows identification of particular classrooms where staff may require additional specialist support or professional development for staff to manage student behavior.
- The accumulation of ODRs for students who share a particular demographic may indicate racism or other forms of prejudice that must be addressed, for staff and students (e.g., disproportionate referrals for students from a particular ethnic group compared with those who are regarded as part of the dominant culture).

- Analyses of ODRs at different grade levels, in different contexts, and for other factors can assist with team problem solving to address challenges (e.g., frequent discipline reports in school hallways and walkways suggests the need for problem solving that might remedy unsafe environments for students).
- Team problem solving using examples of particular types of problem behaviors could lead to the design of schoolwide interventions to address particular issues that appear to be endemic (e.g., incidents of fighting, inappropriate physical contact, assault, abusive language, teasing, and harassment may reveal patterns of bullying requiring systematic attention).
- Ongoing evaluation of ODRs will enable the school to assess the extent to which its approach to educative school discipline is effective and meeting the needs of teachers, children, and the school community.

To achieve these purposes, the formal process for recording behavioral incidents and referrals to the office is an important one, requiring preparation across the school. And again, remember that a system for reporting violations of behavioral expectations anywhere in school cannot be developed in isolation. Effective educative discipline with consequences for problem behavior relies upon the existence of transparent definitions about the school's behavioral expectations (Chapter 2).

What to include in incident reports for ODRs

Once you have clear behavior expectations at your school, the next steps are to define and describe violations of those expectations and clarify what the consequences will be. Just as it was important to reach agreement across the school regarding behavior expectations, there must be agreement across the school about behaviors that do not meet those expectations. This too is a process that requires discussion and negotiation across the school so that school personnel deal with children fairly and consistently and so that children (and their families) perceive they are being treated fairly and consistently.

Table 8 provides an exemplary Incident Report for Office Discipline Referrals that is the result of an extensive consultation process across a school, following detailed consideration to reach consensus about what problem behaviors would be targeted. This system should also differentiate between major and minor transgressions, and reaching consensus on which behaviors fall into each category can be challenging: Failing to discuss these issues across staff and students can lead to ongoing misunderstandings and inconsistencies in application. These in turn reinforce students' feelings of unfairness and even discrimination.

Table 8 Incident Report for Office Discipline Referrals

Incident Report for Office Discipline Referrals (ODR)

Name:	Grade in school:	Referring staff:
Date:	Time of incident:	

Classroom		Restrooms		Administration		Buses
Outside areas		Library		Staffroom		School trips
Hall/walkways		Sports facilities		Auditorium		Other (specify)
Stairwell		School frontage/community		Cafeteria		

(one ✓) Minor problem behavior		(one ✓) Major problem behavior		(one ✓) Actions taken	
Inappropriate language		Abusive language/profanity		Dialogue/conference with student/class	
Inappropriate physical contact		Fighting/physical aggression		Reprimand	
Defiance, disrespect (phone, MP3 player, water bombs)		Defiance/disrespect		Parent contact	
Disruption to class		Disruption to class		Student makes amends	
Lying/cheating		Lying/cheating		Related consequences	
Teasing		Harassment/tease/taunt		Detention	

Property misuse/damage	Lateness (at least 3x)	Demerit
(one ✓) Possible motivation	Forgery/theft	In-school suspension
Obtain peer attention	Skipping class/truancy	
Obtain adult attention	Property misuse/damage	
Obtain item/activities	Substance abuse (drugs, alcohol)	Resolved by
Avoid tasks/activities	Arson	Referring staff
Avoid peer(s)	Weapons	Homeroom teacher Head of Department
Avoid adult	Bomb/fireworks	Dean
Don't know		
(one ✓) Others involved		(Sign)
None	Teacher aide	OR Refer to Senior Management Team (see below)
Peer(s)	Substitute teacher	
Staff	Other_____ (list)	

Other information

1.
2.
3.

Action by Senior Management Team Deputy Principal	Assistant Principal	Principal
	Computer entry	

Source: Adapted with permission from SWIS Referral Form Examples in Todd, Horner, and Dickey (2010).

An incident that meets the definition of either a *minor problem behavior* or a *major problem behavior* requires that the staff member complete the descriptive portion of the incident report and submit it to the school office, even if the incident is managed within the classroom. Basic identifying information including the child's name, year level, date, time of incident, and the referring staff member are entered along with the location where the incident occurred. The incident report is completed by the designated office manager (e.g., the deputy principal who carries schoolwide responsibility for reporting on disciplinary issues) based on information supplied by the referring staff member, the student, and others.

A crucial component of the record is identification of the transgression as a minor problem behavior or a major problem behavior according to agreed definitions that are provided as part of the process. These definitions may be school specific, but they must be transparent to staff, students, and families. The important principle is that the definitions are agreed across the school to ensure disciplinary consistency and fairness. Because some behaviors can be considered to be either minor or major problems (e.g., disruption to class), the definitions must sort these two groups as objectively as possible. Teasing, for example, may be a minor problem behavior if there appeared to be no intent to hurt, but teasing is a major problem behavior if the behaviors escalate, show intent to hurt, and/or evidence racism, sexism, or other forms of prejudice.

Table 9 provides some examples of minor and major problem behaviors along with a sample incident report for ODRs consistent with this list. Our sample incident report includes additional information about possible motivations for the behavior and who else was involved, and space for additional information that might be relevant to understanding what happened. The report also includes a log of the outcome (the behavior consequence for the student), actions taken by the school's senior management team, and initialing by the person completing the report. This too is important, as analyses over time might reveal that previous consequences delivered to particular students would appear to be having no effect when behaviors continue to reoccur regardless of actions taken. These examples have been adapted from those developed for a secondary school in a small town in New Zealand that was implementing SWPBS. While largely an American model (and the examples are "Americanized" with various descriptor terms used in the United States rather than those used in New Zealand), the approach was seen as relevant to New Zealand needs and was found to be useful for the schools that followed this process (Savage, Lewis, & Colless, 2011).

Table 9   Minor Versus Major Behavior Problems in School

Minor Problem Behavior	Major Problem Behavior
Inappropriate language	Abusive language/swearing at others
Inappropriate physical contact	Fighting, assault
Defiance, disrespect (e.g., delayed response)	Defiance, disrespect (e.g., refusals)
Disruption to class (e.g., talking to another student)	Disruption to class (e.g., repeatedly talking out of turn)
Lying/cheating (e.g., asking someone for an answer to a question)	Lying/cheating (e.g., cheating on a final exam, changing one's grade, plagiarism)
Teasing (e.g., one-off humorous remark that does not appear to have hostile intent)	Teasing/harassment (e.g., behaviors unacceptable to recipient, including text bullying, racist remarks, name calling)
Lateness (a few minutes late on more than one occasion)	Lateness (persistent and lengthy lateness without a valid reason)
Property misuse/damage (unintentional breakage through using equipment in an inappropriate area or at inappropriate time)	Property misuse/damage (intentional damage of any kind, including graffiti, and particularly if items are expensive)
	Forgery/theft
	Substance abuse (alcohol, drugs, including failure to report drug possession or supplying at school; possession of drug paraphernalia)
	Weapons (possession of offensive weapon including knife, gun, needle or other object with intent to injure others)
	Bomb threat (including trying to make a bomb)
	Arson (setting fires, possessing lighter or matches in school)

SUICIDE PREVENTION, INTERVENTION, AND POSTVENTION

Suicide is a leading cause of death for young people aged 10–24 in the United States, according to the most recent figures available from the Centers for Disease Control and Prevention (2010). In their survey of members of the National Association of School Psychologists (NASP), Nickerson and Zhe (2004) reported that suicide attempts were among the most frequent crisis events in which school psychologists were involved as part of school crisis response teams (along with student-to-student assault and a student's serious illness or accidental death). And while most suicides involve individual children and youth, it is worth remembering as well that young people responsible for high-profile school shootings have also been suicidal. Clearly, the school psychologist plays a crucial specialist role in evaluating risk, recommending actions, making appropriate referrals, and supporting school, student, and family in suicide prevention and intervention. Nevertheless, the principal has a key supporting role in establishing policy and procedures necessary to ensure that the school and its staff are prepared so that the child who is suicidal, professional personnel, all students, and families receive the appropriate advice and support when there is a crisis.

In 2005, the American School Health Association (ASHA) adopted a resolution calling for schools to include suicide prevention and intervention in their school health program (Poland & Chartrand, 2008), including

1. District policy about student suicide prevention and intervention;

2. Information for all school staff about suicide risk assessment and recognition;

3. Professional development for appropriate school staff about intervention, referral, case management, and aftercare interventions;

4. A school-based crisis intervention team;

5. Clear procedures for school staff to follow when a student threatens or attempts suicide;

6. Collaboration with community health care resources to access mental health services when needed for student, families, and school staff;

7. Safe and effective program(s) for students to address distress, for crisis intervention, and to encourage peer support for seeking help from adults;

8. Strategies to increase school connectedness; and

9. Information and parent training on signs of suicide and accessing resources.

Suicide is rare below age 10, but it does occur. Given the increased risk during adolescence, however, the issue has particular relevance for middle and high school principals. Prevention and intervention programs generally emphasize information for staff about risk factors and warning signs for suicide; basic information for students about recognizing risk, how to respond to a peer, and whom to tell; and appropriate procedures and resource personnel to respond to suicide ideation and threats in school, including involvement of the family.

Very formal programs within schools designed to prevent suicide, such as the Yellow Ribbon program, which is widely accessible to students via Facebook, are controversial. On the one hand, they can encourage the appropriateness of seeking help (the standard Yellow Ribbon message is "It's OK to ask for help"), and they train peers to be responsive to overtures for help and to be sensitive to signs in their friends that teachers, parents, and other adults are likely to miss. On the other hand, they can, when introduced to the school, bring a considerable level of attention, even glamorize, or at least normalize the whole phenomenon of suicide. Another well-known school-based program, Signs of Suicide (SOS), has received some empirical support. When the topic of suicide is formally introduced into the curriculum, usually as part of health studies, the effects are, unfortunately, mixed: While young people's knowledge of suicide issues is increased, there can also be an increase in feelings of hopelessness and maladaptive coping (Ploeg et al., 1996), although other studies have reported no negative effects (Portzky & van Heeringen, 2006). As is so often the case, the conscientious school leader seeking clear guidance from the research literature will find this to be a complex topic and certainly one in which introducing a formal program or protocol and feeling that is sufficient will not prove to be adequate. We believe that the best strategy is to work toward a school atmosphere in which the topic of suicide is not denied; bullying is not tolerated; teachers know and respect their students; students feel able to talk about concerns with teachers and counselors, and their privacy is respected; and students are encouraged to treat each other with empathy and understanding.

Responding to Risk for Student Suicide

A great deal is known empirically about risk factors for suicide. There are demographic and personal characteristics associated with higher rates of suicide: for example, Native Americans and white males have the highest completed suicide rates, while girls and gay, lesbian, and bisexual youth have high rates of attempted suicides. One third to one half of students attempting suicide has depression, and those at risk for suicide exhibit other symptoms such as being pessimistic and having feelings of hopelessness. School-related symptoms include truancy, being suspended, dropping out of school before graduation, low achievement, and school alienation and lack of engagement (Fergusson, Beautrais, & Horwood, 2003). Precipitating events include loss of someone close (through death or break up of a relationship, e.g., with a boyfriend), contagion, being victimized or rejected by peers, failing to achieve valued goals (e.g., low test scores, being rejected for study at a top university after graduation), confusion about sexual identity, and a recent disciplinary event that was humiliating for the student (American Psychological Association, 2004). When thinking of what sorts of students might be especially sensitive to such negative events, it is worth asking if the loss or failure experience challenged a student's cherished ideal. If a student sees herself as popular and likeable, rejection by a boyfriend can threaten her basic view of herself; if a student sees himself as smart and academically successful, an unexpectedly low grade can shatter that self-image.

Debski, Spadafore, Jacob, Poole, and Hixson (2007) report key behavioral warning signs of a potentially suicidal student including the following:

- Increase in drug or alcohol use
- Communicating thoughts of suicide
- Preoccupation with death
- Giving away prized possessions
- Making final arrangements and saying good-bye
- Increased moodiness, withdrawal, or acting out
- Major changes in eating or sleeping habits
- Expressions of hopelessness, guilt, or worthlessness or intense anger toward oneself or others
- Drop in school performance
- Loss of interest in usual activities
- Having a plan for suicide (p. 159)

Whenever a student presents with a number of these signs, Debski et al. emphasize that parental consent is not required for an initial interview with the student as part of assessing for suicide risk. A trained mental health professional such as the school psychologist would generally conduct this interview and carry out the necessary follow through, including contact with the family.

If a student has shown signs of serious risk for suicide, parents should be expected to come to school for a conference, advised to keep a careful watch over their child, remove access to any means of self-harm (e.g., any guns), and seek professional mental health advice from someone with expertise on suicide. When an attempt has been made or threatened, the student should be watched carefully under close supervision until the parents can pick him or her up—and never be sent home alone. If the family seems unwilling to follow up to keep the child safe, Brock and Sandoval (1997) advise they be warned that failure to seek assistance is neglectful and that the school will contact child protective services.

Intervention or Postvention Activities for Suicide

The whole-school response after a completed suicide—termed *postvention* by the American Association of Suicidology—is also important given concerns about suicide contagion and copycat suicide. After a suicide attempt or a completed suicide, there are a number of appropriate procedures to follow so that other students at the school have appropriate support and to prevent the possibility of future, other suicides. There is some evidence of suicide *contagion* or copycat suicides that can occur following a first suicide. Contagion suicide is most likely to occur among close peers, and experts have associated copycat suicides with activities that seem to glamorize or dramatize the suicide though this is not known through empirical research. Schools should plan in advance and have a crisis team in place—trained for any crisis, not just suicide—rather than being reactive and thus being unprepared. The American Association of Suicidology and others recommend the following school response to attempted and completed suicides:

- Verify the suicide report, keep safe the student who attempted suicide, and contact the family, telling them of the school's intervention efforts and offering assistance.
- Notify other students in the school by providing accurate information, being careful not to glamorize or dramatize the suicide situation.
- Notification to the other students should not be through an announcement over the public address system or in an assembly, but rather in one of two ways: (a) if homeroom teachers are knowledgeable and sufficiently well briefed to handle this, have homeroom teachers tell the students what has happened during the same school period; or (b) have an experienced, trained staff member (this could be the school psychologist or a dean) follow the student's

schedule through the day and talk individually with each class group.

- When sharing the information with students, reassure them that the student who attempted suicide is receiving help but keep details about the attempt confidential; encourage students to discuss how to support one another and to express their feelings; acknowledge feelings of responsibility or guilt but emphasize that no one could predict the suicide; and talk about resources for students to get further help if needed.
- Debrief with all school staff, administrators, and crisis response team who dealt with the incident and document all actions taken according to district and school requirements.

Experts advise strongly against cancelling school for the day or helping to organize student attendance at the funeral of a student who has completed suicide (and use the phrase *completed suicide* not *successful* suicide). If possible, the parents could be encouraged to have the funeral outside of school hours so that those who wish to attend can do so. If it is held within school hours, the principal should not provide transportation or cancel classes but should allow those students to attend who wish to do so (Poland & McCormick, 1999).

Immediately after an attempted or completed suicide, school personnel should also be on the alert for signs of suicide contagion or, alternatively, guilt feelings. Additional support should be provided to those close to the student. Virtually all experts and clinicians working in the area of suicide agree that it is important to communicate to others that suicide is not a good solution to problems but be careful not to demean the suicide victim in any way (Brock, 2002).

School Self-Assessment

Table 10 lists true and false statements about suicide prevention and intervention based on available empirical evidence as reported by Debski et al. (2007). School leaders and teachers should be familiar with the correct answers to each statement on the list. The principal also needs to work with appropriate school district personnel to ensure that school policy and procedures are consistent with the evidence on what we know about suicide, rather than being based on what people think or believe is true. We have produced the list with a true/false response column for use by school personnel to test their knowledge on the inventory (correct answers are provided in the last column).

Table 10 Test Your Knowledge About What to Do for Suicide-Related Incidents.

Statement About Suicide	Circle T for True or F for False	Correct Answer
Postvention actions consistent with the literature		
1. Class discussions and literature on teen suicide should be avoided in schools because they may be triggers to suicidal behavior.	T F	False
2. The more detailed the suicide plan, the greater the likelihood the adolescent will complete a suicide.	T F	True
3. If a student is a minor and at risk for suicide, but parents refuse to seek treatment, it is appropriate to warn them that child protective services may be called.	T F	True
4. When it is suspected a student may be suicidal, it is ethically permissible for the psychologist to conduct a risk assessment without first obtaining parental consent.	T F	True
5. The best predictor of a future suicide attempt is a past attempt.	T F	True
6. Research has shown that psychologists can predict suicide attempts with a high degree of accuracy.	T F	False
7. It is never permissible to ask about students' private thoughts and plans without first discussing the boundaries of confidentiality, even if a student may be suicidal.	T F	False
Postvention actions consistent with the literature		
8. The school should identify the death as "accidental" and avoid mention of "suicide" so as to prevent suicide contagion.	T F	False
9. Postvention should begin immediately after the tragedy.	T F	True
10. The school should notify all students of the death by announcement on the public address system.	T F	False
11. The school should verify the facts and treat the death as a suicide.	T F	True

(Continued)

(Continued)

Statement About Suicide	Circle T for True or F for False	Correct Answer
Postvention actions consistent with the literature		
12. The school should provide busing, during school hours, for students who wish to attend funeral services, when consent is given by parents.	T F	False
13. The school should not glorify the death and not allow memorials dedicated to the school victim.	T F	True
What to do/say to a student who is close to another student who has committed suicide		
14. Encourage the student to take control of his or her feelings so as not to get too emotional at school.	T F	False
15. Tell the student that the other student made a foolish decision because he or she was selfish and immature.	T F	False
16. Assure the student that his or her feelings of guilt, anger, grief, and confusion are normal.	T F	True
17. Assure the student that the other student is the only one responsible for his or her actions.	T F	True
18. Assure the student that no one could have foreseen the other student's suicide.	T F	True
19. Remind the student that suicide is a poor choice to solve problems.	T F	True
General school postvention actions consistent with the literature		
20. When interviewed by the media after a student suicide at school, psychologists should disclose what they know about the deceased student and his or her family because the public has a right to know.	T F	False
21. Research suggests that suicide clusters or suicide contagion is a myth.	T F	False
22. After a student suicide, it is better for schools to refer students to a community agency for grief counseling rather than to provide it at school.	T F	False

Source: Adapted from Debski et al. (2007, p. 165).

THREAT ASSESSMENT

One of the difficulties facing teachers, who are then likely to bring their concerns to the principal, is that students may reveal depressive, suicidal, or homicidal thoughts and feelings in their written assignments, creative short stories, art projects, or even doodles on notebooks, tweets, and text messages to friends. It is fairly easy to dismiss these as normal childhood or adolescent preoccupation with morbid, Gothic topics, but the reality is that well-adjusted young people do not spend large amounts of time focused obsessively on themes of death, violence, guns, and other weapons. It would be sensible, therefore, not to dismiss teacher concerns as overreacting and to encourage teachers who alert you to these sorts of expression to talk to the student calmly and to probe, without feeling shocked or anxious, where these morbid preoccupations might be coming from, including family violence and experiences of physical or sexual abuse. Sometimes the statements made by students (or adults) in schools may go beyond ordinary verbal aggression or harassment (whether minor or major), such as threats of future violence that are alarming and frightening. The occurrence of tragedies such as the shootings at Columbine High School in Colorado in 1999, Red Lake High School in Minnesota in 2005, the Amish school in Pennsylvania in 2006, and Virginia Tech University in 2007 emphasize the role of *threat assessment* in preventing violence in schools, where there are large concentrations of children and adults who can be at risk. Threat assessment was originally developed by the U.S. Secret Service to identify risk to public officials from verbal and/or written threats to commit a violent act against prominent figures and others (Strong & Cornell, 2008).

Threat assessment is different from *profiling*, which that labels characteristics of people likely to commit violence. Hence it would be inappropriate to decide that a particular student has characteristics that make him or her dangerous to others without additional evidence of intent to harm. Threat assessment is *in response to a person's specific threatening behavior.* In addition, threat assessment requires a judgment about whether the person who has made a threat *is actually likely to carry out the threat.*

Every school leader will be familiar with what are sometimes called *empty* threats, shouted in the heat of the moment. Threats such as "I'll teach him a lesson" or "You'll get yours" represent verbal behaviors that are socially unacceptable and will generally lead to consequences as well as hard feelings and even fear. But some threats using the very same words may actually foreshadow violence and harm that could have been prevented had those words been taken seriously.

Cornell and Sheras (2006) have written a useful and practical set of *Guidelines for Responding to Student Threats of Violence* and provide a definition of a threat:

What Is a Threat?

A threat is **an expression of intent to harm someone.** Threats may be spoken, written, or expressed in some way, such as through gestures. Threats may be direct ("I am going to beat you up") or indirect ("I'm going to get him"). Illegal possession of weapons should be presumed to indicate a threat unless careful investigation reveals otherwise (e.g., a student accidentally brought a knife to school). When in doubt about whether a student's behavior is a threat, evaluate it as a threat. (p. 1)

School personnel need clear and practical guidelines for identifying threats that could lead to committing an act of violence; remember too that threats may be made by students but also by staff members. Whenever a person verbally threatens violence or engages in behavior suggesting violence (e.g., pulling out a knife), threat assessment must be carried out urgently about whether the threat is likely to be carried out.

A joint report (Fein et al., 2002) of the U.S. Secret Service and the U.S. Department of Education described six principles for investigating potentially dangerous threats:

1. Targeted school violence can be prevented if attention is paid to early warning signs: someone who commits violence will think about, plan, and even discuss threats with others over a period of time—not suddenly "snap."

2. Context is important, including both the circumstances and peer group influences on the person making the threat and the situation in which the threat is made; threatening words may actually be a bad joke or reflect a rhetorical remark, not an actual intent to commit violence.

3. Be skeptical and investigative about threats rather than jumping to conclusions based on thinking someone is inclined to violence. There can be a tendency for some school personnel to exaggerate rumors about someone or even act on secondhand information against a student who has done nothing but may be disliked by others.

4. Rely on facts to make your final judgment, not what you think the person "is like" as this is not profiling based on characteristics but assessment based on objective information.

5. Gather information from more than one source, including interviewing others around the person who made the threat (e.g.,

friends) and checking with relevant community agency personnel such as law enforcement, social workers, mental health providers, religious organizations, and others. You can do this on a confidential basis and need to do this if the threat appears to be a serious one.

6. Keep the focus on whether the student *poses a threat*, not whether the student *made a threat*. Threat assessment is all about how serious the threat is and what should be done about it, not whether the threat was made in the first place.

Having robust procedures for threat assessment is also an alternative to *zero-tolerance* approaches that can lead to harsh and inappropriate punishment. There are, for example, documented cases of children expelled for doing things like bringing a toy gun to school, giving the teacher a razor blade found on the street, and having a manicure kit that included a tiny knife (Skiba & Peterson, 1999).

Cornell and Sheras (2006) suggest the following steps for threat assessment:

Step 1: Evaluate the threat. The school leader interviews the student making the threat and any witnesses and considers context and meaning along with literal content.

Step 2: Decide whether the threat is transient or substantive. A transient threat is not serious and can easily be resolved while a *substantive* threat involves the risk of potential injury to others.

Step 3: If the threat is transient, respond using disciplinary procedures such as reprimand, parent notification, etc., appropriate to severity and chronicity of the incident.

Step 4: If the threat is substantive, is it serious or very serious? A threat to hit, assault, or beat up someone is serious, whereas a threat to kill, rape, use a weapon, or injure someone severely is very serious.

Step 5: Respond to a serious substantive threat by taking action to prevent violence including notifying potential victims and addressing the conflict or problem associated with the threat. This completes the process for a serious substantive threat.

Step 6: Respond to a very serious substantive threat (conduct a safety evaluation) by taking immediate protective action, including contacting law enforcement, removing the student, and completing a safety evaluation including a mental health assessment to determine referral and support needs.

Step 7: Implement a safety plan to protect potential victims and meet the student's educational needs. (p. 17)

Whenever you become aware of threatening behavior, in which another individual's safety might be compromised, you will be faced with a number of ethical dilemmas, of which the most complex is typically around confidentiality and the student's right to privacy. Students may well approach teachers or a school leader such as the principal with a serious concern and will request total confidentiality prior to disclosure ("I'm going to tell you about something, but you must first promise not to breathe a word of this to anyone, especially my parents."). Professional counselors, psychologists, and other mental health experts are now well aware that they cannot give such an assurance to any client. There is a well-established principle in counseling called "the duty to warn" (the potential victim or anyone who might be harmed by the disclosure), which is better expressed as "the duty to prevent." Counselors (including teachers) will often agonize over this, since without giving the reassurance to complete confidentiality, they know that the young person may then not report suicidal thoughts, homicidal ideation, rape, pregnancy, a crime committed, or any of a number of secrets with negative consequences. On the other hand, the counselor, who is not like a priest in the confessional, has a responsibility to society and to members of the public to alert them to dangers and to ensure that any harm is prevented. School personnel, therefore, need to explain the limits to confidentiality and the situations that would require them to breach confidentiality—usually when there is a risk to the person themselves or to another individual being harmed. Remember that to keep a young person safe in a variety of situations, parents and family members may need to be informed and brought into the restorative process, no matter how much the young person might resist this at first, through embarrassment, shame, fear of retribution, and fear of consequences for the family member. In a positive, proactive, restorative culture, it is actually easier to convince a student that it is only through an open, honest, and nonconfrontational or nonlitigious approach that real solutions can be negotiated.

MANAGING ASSAULTS AND BREAKING UP FIGHTS

At least two to three members of the senior leadership team of any school should be well trained in and confident of their ability to intervene in a fight when events are out of control. It is a reality in schools that many students—even during the elementary school years—experience violence in their lives and have seen, participated in, or been the victims of a physical fight that goes beyond rough and tumble play. The first step in preventing violence is, of course, to avoid it. The principal and all school personnel should have basic skills and understandings of nonviolent crisis intervention, particularly nonconfrontational language that they use reliably when faced with a potentially dangerous situation or a problem about to happen. For example, a teacher may observe two students facing one another with aggressive postures, and what that teacher says can either inflame or defuse the situation. Staff must also make judgments about whether students are still in control of their own emotions or if they are so aroused that talk alone is unlikely to have the desired effect. Wolfgang (2005, pp. 267–268) describes "six steps to problem solving":

- *Step 1*: Defining the problem and getting the student to acknowledge that there is a problem
- *Step 2*: Generating possible solutions and asking the student to come up with positive ways to solve the problem
- *Step 3*: Evaluating the solutions to examine the likely results of trying different approaches to solving the problem
- *Step 4*: Deciding which solution is best with the student acknowledging that decision
- *Step 5*: Implementing the (best) solution
- *Step 6:* Evaluating whether it worked for the student and solved the problem

School leaders will know that matching student violence or aggression with staff aggression and even shouting may do no more than escalate the situation further. In some situations, allowing a student to vent may be a good choice for the staff member rather than demanding that the student be compliant and stop talking immediately. In other instances, the verbal aggression may be building toward physical attack—so good judgment is essential.

Once a teacher has determined that he or she needs to interrupt a potentially dangerous situation, how this is done is crucial. In the early phases of an aggressive incident, Wolfgang suggests that *supportive demands* are best and provides guidelines for these that are described in more detail in *The Teacher's Guide*. If violence has occurred, however, an adult may be required to intervene physically to protect self and others. Just as any school should have a critical mass of staff who are trained in first aid, there should be a critical mass of staff who are trained in techniques to prevent and intervene with violence. Staff require training in how to interrupt and contravene physical assaults such as choking, biting, kicking, and hitting as well as how to use nonviolent restraint and when and how to transport a student from one location to a safer one (Wolfgang, 2005).

A STANDARD EMERGENCY RESPONSE
PROTOCOL (SERP) FOR SCHOOL SAFETY

Another issue important for school safety is to have in place a schoolwide, classroom response to any incident that might occur at school and place children and adults at risk. These incidents might be weather events, fires, accidental explosions, and intruders who enter the school grounds with the expressed intent of doing harm and/or use the school as a sanctuary and those in the school as hostages.

Preparing for natural disasters is fairly common in schools: Virtually all schools have regular fire drills, and schools in severe weather areas will have tornado and hurricane drills. Adults who were children in school in the 1950s will even recall drills to prepare for the event of a nuclear attack, for which preparation consisted of stooping under one's desk (hardly effective against a nuclear missile!). The September 11, 2001, attacks in New York City and various shooting incidents involving armed intruders entering school grounds with apparent intent to kill randomly have also raised awareness of the potential for almost random harm.

Given the potential for incidents to occur with minimal or even no advance notice, school personnel need to have a plan for everyone on the school grounds regarding how to respond at the first signs of trouble—and how to signal to everyone at school that a response is needed. Prothrow-Stith (1987) makes a strong case for teaching children directly how to keep themselves safe by learning how to prevent conflicts from escalating, how to defuse anger (their own and others'), how to recognize dangerous situations, and how to avoid weapons. Martella, Nelson, and Marchand-Martella (2003) advocate that school leaders should determine which threats are possible for a particular school and ensure that all members of the school community would know what to do should an incident occur. This preparation is relevant at school level for events such as severe storms or invasion by an armed intruder and at classroom level for violent outbursts or suicide threats. Key to this preparation is the establishment of a simple and effective communication system that is well understood by all and thus will work in a crisis. The principal should, for example, establish processes that each individual teacher can and would use if there were a serious incident in his or her classroom so that help would arrive within minutes.

Ellen Stoddard-Keyes of the National School Safety Collaborative (NSSC) has developed an umbrella program for school safety and awareness-based activities supported by the "I Love U Guys" Foundation (Community First Foundation, 2009). As part of this program, a Standard Response Protocol (SRP) has been developed as a recipe for safe schools that rehearses specific classroom responses to an incident. The SRP incorporates four specific responses to a threatening incident:

1. *Lockout*: Securing the school/building's outside perimeter

2. *Lockdown*: Securing individual rooms and keeping students quiet and in place

3. *Evacuate*: Orderly movement of students and staff from one (unsafe) location to a different (safe) location in or out of the building

4. *Shelter*: Self-protection followed by a method that has been rehearsed and may be carried out by particular designated individuals in school

SUMMARY

This chapter covers decision making by school leaders toward the development of transparent and fair guidelines for how the school responds to behaviors and incidents. It discusses judgments about the seriousness of behavior that reflect whether or not behavior causes or has the potential to harm others, as well as its effects on the child who exhibits the behavior. Specific procedures are introduced that can perform multiple reporting, data monitoring, and effectiveness evaluation purposes in supporting restorative school discipline. Guidelines are also included regarding intervening in conflict situations where individual students have caused harm or there is a threat to safety. The procedures described in the chapter fit within an overall preventative school ethos of restorative school discipline with fair and transparent consequences for identified behavior and incidents in a manner designed to ensure safety for everyone in the school environment.

6 Restorative Conferencing and In-School Suspension

This chapter focuses on consequences when serious behavior and serious incidents that require a response from the principal at the level of the school occur. Regardless of how fair and supportive the setting, there are times when children engage in serious behaviors that can and do cause harm to themselves and others. Remember that the purpose of having clear, well-designed consequences is both to stop an ongoing behavior and to reduce the risk of the behavior reoccurring in the future. This chapter addresses the kinds of consequences that must be in place for very serious behavior within schools that are committed to positive approaches such as restorative school discipline. We describe the process of restorative conferencing recommended for use by the school principal in response to serious incidents. The chapter also provides details about how to establish a system of in-school suspension as a consequence for serious behavior that might have otherwise led to out-of-school suspension.

RESTORATIVE PRACTICES FOR SERIOUS INCIDENTS

In Chapter 5, we introduced processes to record the range of behaviors and incidents that can occur in schools. In addition to the systems schools may use to record incidents and individual behaviors that present challenges for staff and students, school districts and schools generally have in place a set of requirements and guidelines regarding suspensions and exclusions whereby students are required to leave school temporarily or even permanently. Schools typically have permanent records and formal processes for suspending students for serious behaviors. Across schools, referrals and suspensions may not be objectively similar or proportionately equal but may vary greatly. This variation reflects actual differences in challenging behaviors, cultural mismatches between school and community, and/or the extent to which school personnel have the necessary skills and understandings to manage behavior.

Nevertheless, there are differences between schools with high versus low rates of behavioral challenges. Schools with low suspension rates have the following characteristics:

- The school climate is positive, and children feel safe and emotionally secure in classrooms.
- Teachers and other school personnel hold positive images of students and their families.
- There are high levels of engagement and participation by students in school activities.
- The school follows proactive and preventive discipline approaches rather than being oriented toward punishment.
- There is a transparent discipline policy with clear definitions of behavior expectations and what the consequences would be for breaking the code of conduct.
- The levels of parental involvement are high.

Each of these characteristics requires more explicit and objective definition for both staff and students. Section I of this guide covers the features of a positive school climate and the framework for restorative school discipline. Chapters 3 to 5 provide further details regarding decision making about minor versus major problem behavior, including information regarding different needs that will require additional support services for children and their families.

Consequences for Serious Incidents Within Restorative Practices

There will be times when behavior is severe so that suspension is the required natural consequence for that behavior. Even when removal from the classroom or playground is necessary for protection, it is important that the processes for doing so are transparent and fair so that the end result improves the situation rather than exacerbates difficulties. Traditional punishment approaches can actually add to existing hostility for offenders and exaggerate fear or anger for victims. Thus, when suspension is required for serious incidents, consequences must be delivered to those students who do not meet behavioral expectations without sacrificing their sense of belonging and personal dignity during the process of restoration. This is in keeping with the old concept in parenting that the parent dislikes the behavior, not the child, and it is the behavior that is being consequated.

The Teacher's Guide describes classroom conferencing procedures for both prevention of conflict and intervention for minor incidents before things get out of hand. Throughout the different school contexts, participants in conflict have opportunities to practice reflection and develop skills in mediation. In Chapter 3, we covered restorative curricula and the different levels of restorative conferencing for prevention including restorative language and scripts, restorative inquiry, restorative conversations, and the use of meetings and conferences by teachers at the classroom level. We also introduced the ongoing systems that should be in place across the school to support students and staff, including mediation. More detail about these procedures for teachers is provided in the series' companion, *Teacher's Guide to Restorative Classroom Discipline*. These procedures mean that, in a school committed at all levels to restorative school discipline, students will have many opportunities to develop basic understandings about restorative practices and the importance of listening to different perspectives. Thus, even students who display high levels of challenging behavior should nevertheless be aware that their point of view will be heard and considered, which contrasts with more traditional disciplinary processes where the staff's and victims' sides of the story tend to dominate.

This chapter complements prevention processes and individualized child-intervention approaches described in earlier sections of this guide in providing details about how school leaders respond to major behavioral incidents. Restorative conferencing is described, including negotiation of appropriate follow-up and consequences. Restorative processes require that all participants in conflict are heard. They also require everyone to review and disclose information that could assist in problem solving—going beyond simply listing the behavior of the student that caused concern to describe events leading up to that behavior and reflect on the situation. Reconciliation of all parties is encouraged through individual and then coconstructed review of incidents leading up to discipline and consequences. In restorative school discipline, the guiding principles of restoration and valuing of inclusion signify the need for alternatives to exclusion and punishment. These alternatives must be aligned with opportunities to make amends while also protecting the safety of the school community and delivering natural consequences for serious behavior in a way that does not further disadvantage and alienate the student from the school community. The first step in this process is a formal conference.

RESTORATIVE SCHOOL CONFERENCES

In Chapter 3, we described restorative practices curricula across the grades and the different levels of restorative conferencing for prevention, including restorative language and scripts, restorative inquiry, restorative conversations, and the use of meetings and conferences by teachers and at the classroom level. We also introduced the ongoing systems that should be in place across the school to support students and staff, including mediation. More detail about these procedures for teachers is provided in the series' companion *Teacher's Guide to Restorative Classroom Discipline*. Here, we describe the procedures for formal conferences that are needed when serious offenses take place that cause harm and/or represent a threat to the safety of others.

Traditionally, serious offenses have resulted in immediate suspension and exclusion without a great deal of conversation involving either the offender or the victim other than a review of what happened. In restorative school discipline, the guiding principles of restoration and valuing of inclusion signify the need for alternative approaches that protect the safety of others, align with the requirement to make amends, and also deliver natural consequences for serious behavior in a way that does not further disadvantage and alienate the student from his or her school community. The first step in this process is to set up a formal conference. Within a restorative practices approach to school discipline, in-school suspension might commence at the same time as the decision is made to set up the formal conference—or a decision flowing from the conference might be that the offending student must spend time in the in-school suspension room as part of the restoration process. These are decisions made by the school principal at the time of the report, in accordance with guidelines that are well known throughout the school among staff, students, families, and the school community generally.

The Facilitator Role in Restorative Conferences

Each school should have determined in advance who the facilitator will be for formal conferences triggered by serious incidents. If the facilitator is someone from within the school, having more than one senior leader prepared to facilitate means that a choice can be made when the need arises regarding who is available and most appropriate in a particular case. The trained facilitator team might include the deputy or vice principal, dean, and senior teacher(s) who have received training in facilitation; generally, the most appropriate facilitator in a given case will be someone who is not involved directly in the student's educational program. We recommend that the school principal not be the person who facilitates restorative school conferences, as this could result in a conflict of commitment for the principal's role as he or she has multiple responsibilities beyond the conference. Another possibility is to contract the services of a trained independent consultant specifically for this purpose on an as-needed basis. Finally, the school psychologist or counselor could serve as facilitator, but this could become complicated if that person is already providing services to the offender so that there could be perceptions of advocacy or a conflict of interest.

In their comprehensive evaluation of the large-scale implementation of restorative practices in Scottish schools, Kane et al. (2007) reported that use of formal conferencing was limited where prevention activities were well developed. When formal conferences were held at either elementary or secondary schools, the nature of the incident and the skill of the facilitator influenced whether staff perceived the conference to have been successful. One teacher described how a trained facilitator met with a group of 20 students and their elementary teacher to address racist remarks overheard in class. She felt that the students developed a good understanding of how hurtful such remarks can be and the conference had been a more effective way of dealing with the problem rather than traditional disciplinary procedures.

Formal conferencing can be challenging, particularly as it requires conversations that differ from the usual punitive and judgmental speeches that often occur in schools between adults and students. Whenever a serious incident has occurred, there will be an undercurrent of injustice and blame along with strong feelings by at least some of the participants that the offender needs to be "taught a lesson" or "brought into line." Conferencing requires new ways of speaking respectfully to everyone and in ways that promote discussion rather than lecturing or asserting authority about the rules. In secondary schools in particular, conferencing will not be effective if students refuse to participate or use the conference as a forum to pursue the original argument or conflict. Participants can be insincere and just say what they know others want to hear, and an offending student may be able to manipulate the conference dialogue to avoid accepting responsibility and making amends. If the offending student isn't showing empathy for the victim, proceeding with a conference could actually be detrimental if it becomes a second forum to victimize the victim further. Hence, the facilitator's role is crucial both in setting up the conference and in ensuring that participants are in a proper frame of mind for the conference to work.

Guidelines for a Formal Conference

In Canada, in the juvenile justice system, the restorative conference recognizes that no matter what the outcome of the process, there will be an ongoing interaction between the alleged offender and his or her victim and their extended families. As used with Aboriginal communities in the Yukon, the conference is sometimes called a *sentencing circle*. It is literally a circle of concerned community members, providing a safe voice for all persons affected by the offending behavior. Its three core principles are in keeping with cultural traditions of the indigenous people, namely (a) that a criminal offense represents a breach of the relationship between the offender and the victim, as well as the offender and the community; (b) the future stability of the community is dependent on healing these rifts; and (c) that the community is in a better position to recognize the complex causes of offender behavior and their connection with economic and social disadvantage as well as other concerns such as addictions and community anger at lost resources, broken promises, and past abuses. Bateman and Berryman (2008) describe four core concepts that have been used in successful adaptations of restorative conference practices with indigenous students incorporating similar collectivist cultural values:

1. *Reaching consensus* about the problem through restorative listening and collaborative decision making by participants in the conference

2. *Reconciliation* in reaching an agreement about moving forward that is acceptable to everyone involved rather than punitive and that allows repair of relationships damaged by the events or incident

3. *Examination* of the broader context that may have contributed to the incident and harm, including acceptance of responsibility by all parties rather than focusing on agreement that one person was solely to blame

4. *Restoration* of positive relationships and how to maintain positive relationships in the future, which is more important than emphasizing past breaches or mistakes

We'll use an actual incident that occurred in a middle school to illustrate the process of a formal restorative conference. This event is fairly typical of verbal and physical conflict in secondary schools, and it could be instigated by a student who is already identified as having a behavioral disorder—as is the case for TJ in the example—or by any student or students who might be provoked by what appears to be an insignificant event.

Planning for a Restorative School Conference

The first step in planning for a restorative school conference is, of course, the decision that a formal conference is the way forward. TJ has already had difficulties in his new school, and things seem to be escalating rather than settling in. The principal as school leader decides to start the

The Incident: Physical Violence in Middle School

TJ: TJ is a 13-year-old male student in Grade 9 attending a large middle school. He is relatively new to the school, having arrived only two months ago; he was expelled from another school for fighting. He appears to be doing slightly below average work in most curriculum areas with the exception of English, where he is performing well, and the teacher says he has a talent for writing. Since being at the new middle school, he has been having the following difficulties: (a) poor attendance; (b) returning from lunch smelling of alcohol and, when confronted by the teacher, angrily denying drinking; (c) failing to complete any homework; and (d) reports of intimidation from peers, including reported threats to "beat you up" happening in the hallways though no incidents had been observed directly by an adult. In two months, he has had three previous office referrals from three different teachers for shouting in the classroom. He doesn't seem to have any friends at school but is reported to hang out in the neighborhood with boys from his previous school who also have problems.

Background: TJ was diagnosed some years ago as having attention deficit/hyperactivity disorder and has been receiving special education support services from a school psychologist for aggression and defiance. Previous serious behaviors noted in his records include numerous altercations with peers, being one of three boys accused of setting a fire in a wastepaper basket in an empty classroom, and talking back to teachers. He was accused of smoking dope last year, but this wasn't documented. He is considered to be of average intelligence, talks a lot, and seems to ooze confidence. He is also described as having an uncanny ability to get others to reveal things about themselves that he later uses to embarrass them in front of others or to get even.

The Incident Report: The incident occurred during math class. The teacher was collecting the previous night's homework from students. When she got to TJ, he said he didn't have his while rocking on two legs of his chair. The teacher told him to stop that and pressed him about why he didn't have the work. TJ said he "just didn't feel like doing it." The teacher replied something to the effect that "That isn't good enough, and I'd expect a better answer from you than that." Another male student (Sam) laughed, and TJ said loudly, "So what's so funny?" Sam made a face, then turned his back and didn't answer. After school that day, TJ waited at the fence and grabbed Sam when he walked by. TJ is reported to have verbally confronted Sam; a loud argument ensued, followed by TJ kicking Sam and hitting him with his fists. Sam has bruises on his left leg and both forearms. Sam's father reported the incident later that same afternoon after Sam arrived home. TJ was called into the office the next morning by the principal and responded that Sam got what he deserved for laughing at him.

process for a formal conference based on the circumstances surrounding TJ's presence in the school and this specific incident. Deciding to proceed with a formal conference should always be consistent with existing school policies and procedures. In this example, the principal would have consulted with the math teacher and other teachers who know both boys in determining how to proceed; in particular, he might speak with the English teacher given TJ's reported strengths in that subject. The reference in the files to negative peer influences from his old school and the lack of any friends in the new school might also be issues for the principal to explore with teachers before the conference.

In most schools, an incident such as this one would require notice to the school board regardless of whether a restorative conference is held. This notice would include assurances that student safety will not be compromised during the interim planning period, and TJ is likely to be assigned immediately after the incident to in-school suspension (see procedures described later in this chapter) with the length of that suspension determined following the conference. The formal conference requires organization, significant time commitment from all participants, and resources—particularly if an external consultant is contracted to facilitate. Hence, one useful rule of thumb for determining when a conference is indicated could be that the incident is serious enough that suspension or expulsion would be the consequence under normal circumstances. It is also crucial that all participants are prepared to engage in restorative language at the conference, and Drewery (2004) has summarized the vital role of restorative, not retributive, conversations based on extensive experience with formal conferencing in New Zealand schools.

A key participant is the victim: for most incidents leading to a school conference, there will be a victim, but note that designated victims are not always themselves totally innocent. In this case, it is Sam. It is desirable for the victim to be part of the conference provided he or she can be made to feel safe. In some cases, the victim may be unable or unwilling to attend. It can still be productive to proceed with a formal conference, but if the victim doesn't attend personally, the victim's perspective must be brought into the meeting by a representative or perhaps by letter or a recording. It may also be that the victim has deliberately or otherwise played an important role in the incident. The principal should be interested in the fact that Sam's laughter was the antecedent to TJ's anger: this may not be the first time, and it's possible that TJ is being ridiculed by other students. Peer relationships at school are important, so knowing more about how well TJ is getting along with peers and whether there has been any previous conflict with Sam in particular could provide critical information for the conference. Finally, if the victim's main agenda is to see to it that the offender is punished and is made to suffer, it will not be productive to have that person at a formal conference (Drewery, 2004).

The willingness of the offender to participate in good faith must also be taken into account. If the offender seems most interested in blaming someone else and not willing to listen to different perspectives, it will not be helpful to initiate the conference until after preliminary discussions have worked through such issues. It is not advisable for a conference to proceed whenever the offender shows no interest in making amends; this stance indicates that further individualized intervention or therapy is needed before the conference can proceed. Even after a conference begins, it may become clear that the groundwork hasn't been laid for positive restoration and the tone is instead sounding like a disciplinary hearing. If this happens, the facilitator may—in consultation with the principal—abandon the process at least temporarily.

There are four distinct phases to a restorative school conference:

1. *Preparation*: As noted above, it is important to ensure that all participants—including the offender and victim(s)—are willing to participate in the conference and to go along with what is decided. Obtaining everyone's agreement may require a series of conversations with different parties separately—similar to shuttle mediation—prior to the formal meeting. Everyone who participates in the conference must be part of this, but it is particularly crucial that the offender TJ and his victim Sam are not forced to be part of the conference but participate voluntarily. It is possible that several conversations are needed before the two boys will agree, and a trained facilitator will engage in this negotiation in a manner that reassures both offender and victim that the purpose of the meeting is to make amends, restore, and move forward—not to blame or leave anyone feeling shamed or victimized.

2. *The conference*: The conference should be held in a somewhat neutral setting, neither in the school office nor in the mathematics classroom where the incident occurred but in another room that has no prior associations. It should be scheduled outside the school day so that both family members and school personnel do not have competing obligations. Realistically, 90 minutes should be allowed for the meeting, and food and drink should be provided at the start. The conference begins with less formal sharing of refreshments (perhaps juice and cookies), and the facilitator invites participants to introduce themselves individually with each person stating one thing he or she would like to happen as a result of the conference. More details will be provided in the next section regarding the agenda and process for the conference itself.

3. *Forming a plan*: Once the conference has concluded, a formal plan must be developed to make amends and restore damaged relationships. The plan most often will include the initial period of in-school suspension as well, along with conditions for returning to the mathematics classroom. The plan would address longer term issues for TJ (working with the school psychologist and his teachers) and would also deal with any lingering safety concerns (e.g., student fears about lack of supervision near the school groups making Sam and other students vulnerable to future attacks). The plan must also specify outcome evidence that will be monitored in order to make future judgments about its effectiveness. The series companion *Consultant's Guide* includes details about conference follow-up plans.

4. *Follow-up and review*: Whenever there has been a serious incident, a restorative school conference, and an intervention plan, there must also be follow-up and review to evaluate outcomes for restoring relationships and making amends for the participants involved. We recommend follow-up within 3 to 6 months of the incident, and information gathered for the follow-up evaluation should be used to revise and modify program plans for students who require ongoing support.

For the incident involving TJ, the key participants for a formal conference will be TJ and Sam along with their support persons—including at least family members—and others involved in the incident, especially the math teacher. The offender and the victim should each be given the option of having someone at the meeting with them in addition to family members. In our example, TJ's mom is available, but his father lives out of town and cannot participate; his mom also invites her brother (TJ's uncle) to come as she feels he has more influence on TJ than she does. TJ says he doesn't want to invite a friend, but when asked whether there is anyone else at school he'd like to invite, he does express interest in having the English teacher come along (whom he seems to like and who has encouraged him to write). Both Sam's mother and father are available, and Sam also wants to invite Mitchell from the mathematics class and a friend, Jeremy, as well because he was witness to the attack. The mathematics teacher must also be there as the adult who was witness to and even part of the incident. The principal or deputy who managed the incident and will report what happened at the start of the conference must also be present. Finally, as TJ is in the process of being reassessed for behavioral support services, the school psychologist should attend.

Conferencing Questions

Once participants have shared some food and drink, conference introductions are made with each person indicating what he or she would like to result from the conference. This will give the facilitator clues about whether key participants are in a frame of mind for a useful restorative conference. Next, the facilitator invites the principal or deputy from the school to describe the incident: This role cannot be performed by the facilitator and ideally is done by a school leader whose responsibility is to record events and incidents as they happened. The reporter (i.e., principal or deputy) gives an objective and balanced reporting of the incident. This report might be read straight from the incident report, but it is important to omit emotive language and attributions that suggest underlying causes or hostility. That is more difficult than it sounds. As a practice, try giving a neutral but accurate description of the TJ incident. Where would you start? Would you start with the noncompletion of homework, TJ's response to the teacher, Sam's laughter, or TJ's attack on Sam? If you say, "Sam laughed at TJ," Sam might be able to blurt out, "I didn't laugh at him; I laughed at how he was getting the better of Ms. M."

Essentially, you will need a description that no one in the room will immediately contradict. As this description is the first step in reporting what happened, when the facts are presented, it is not the time to engage in argument or disagreement about the incident itself. To ensure this, therefore, it would be important, prior to the conference, for the principal to have heard out both TJ (the offender) and Sam (the victim), as well as anyone else directly involved in the incident, so that the information included in the incident report is as complete as possible. This objective description should be forthright about the seriousness of the incident. The facilitator first asks the victim to agree if this is a fair account of what happened, and then the offender is asked the same question. Finally, the student who has committed the offense should indicate willingness to make amends—and the conference can proceed.

The group then continues with responses to the key questions. In Chapter 3, we describe the generic restorative practices questions that form the core for conferencing. We have adapted the following set of key questions based on guidelines developed by the Restorative Practices Development Team (2003) to keep the focus of the conference on the specific issues:

- What happened? What led to the incident?
- Why is the school considering serious disciplinary consequences?
- Does everyone accept that the explanation given is a fair account of what happened?
- What was each person thinking when he or she did what he or she did?

- Was there a difference between what happened and what each person intended?
- Is each person willing to try to make amends in order to set things right?

These questions could be displayed on a whiteboard during the conference so that the facilitator can refer to them if necessary in order to keep the conversation from wandering into areas that are not relevant.

Mapping the Problem and Its Effects

The Restorative Practices Development Team (2003) suggests that the next step is to draw a map that includes naming the problem and its effects. Figure 1 illustrates the two stages of this mapping process for TJ.

Figure 1 Mapping the Problem for TJ

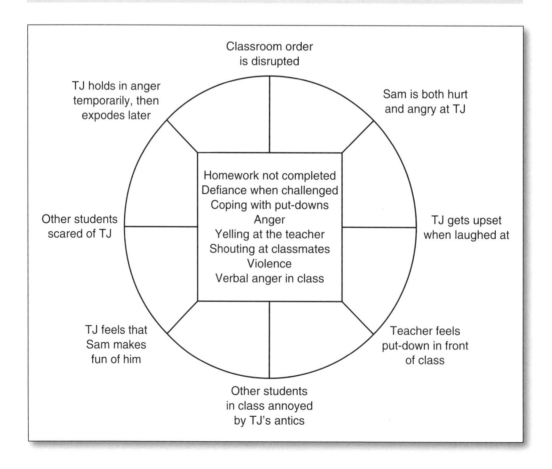

First, the facilitator draws a box in the middle of a wheel on the whiteboard and invites everyone to suggest words or phrases that describe the problem or aspects of the problem that will be listed in this box. The list for TJ includes input from the teacher (homework not completed; yelling at the teacher) and others (defiance when challenged, violence). Note that none of the problem statements make comments about the offender but focus on the behavior or thoughts. Thus, the phrase *verbal anger in class* is recorded rather than something like *hostile nature*. Remember that the fundamental attribution fallacy is to focus on psychological traits rather than context as an explanation for behavior, so make a special effort to identify the situational variables. When the list of possible aspects of the problem is completed, the facilitator highlights that everything on the list is actually part of the problem and that there is no reason to agree on a single way or name for the problem as all the multiple perspectives are important to acknowledge. The group could decide to focus on which ones are priorities for the meeting, but this doesn't mean that the other perspectives are not valid.

Next, each participant should be given the opportunity to express the effects of the problem on him or her. The facilitator uses the spokes emanating outward from the center of the wheel to put different perspectives at the end of each spoke, always asking the victim to speak first. If the victim is initially hesitant, a support person could make the first statement about effects on the victim, and then the facilitator could give Sam another opportunity to add effects. The facilitator should give Sam repeated opportunities by asking probe questions such as "How else has it affected you?" and "What else has happened to you because of this problem?" Others are then invited to contribute effects, such as the teacher, Sam's friends, and family members. The offender must also be given the opportunity to name how the problem has affected him.

For our example incident, eight *effects* have been recorded from conference participants. Effects can be

- Feelings such as anger, fear, embarrassment
- Physical results such as bruises, cuts, scratches, headaches
- Reactions such as hostile thoughts or intentions to avoid school
- Actions or behaviors such as interruptions to class activities
- Social outcomes such as negative relationships, friendships ending

Mapping Solutions

Another map (see Figure 2) is created next to work out possible solutions to the problem.

Figure 2 Mapping Solutions for TJ

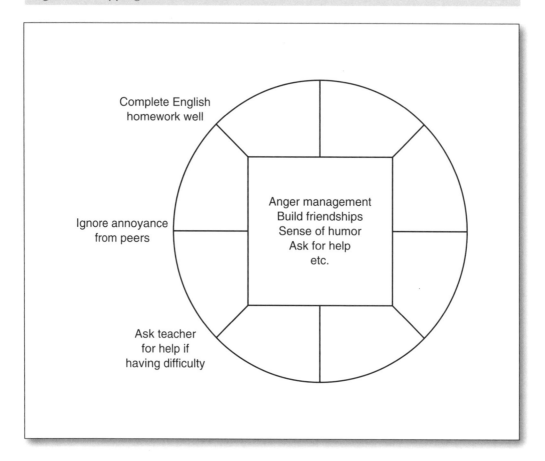

This time, the facilitator draws an empty middle circle with all its spokes, leaving the middle circle empty but asking participants to fill in the space at the end of the different spokes that should record exceptions to problem behavior. For example, Sam might be asked if he can think of a time when he had a different, more neutral or even friendly interaction with TJ. The English teacher might give an example when TJ had completed his work and done well. TJ might describe how he approached the teacher politely on another occasion when he hadn't finished homework and a time when he was able to ignore a peer who was annoying him in some way. After filling in these *positive alternative* boxes, the facilitator asks participants to name the qualities or characteristics that might lead to those more positive alternatives. This process could then result in filling in the center circle with phrases like "anger management," "build friendships," "sense of humor," and "ask for help." The offender would then be asked whether he thinks he has the skills and self-control to do all of those things.

Essentially, the two maps tell two stories. One story—the one leading to the incident—is a description of the current problem and the effects of that problem on participants. The second story is one that is already happening to some extent but that needs to develop further to grow the skills and understandings needed to prevent future incidents and build positive relationships. The facilitator should point this out and ask everyone to focus on the next step, which is to decide what needs to happen next to change the first story to the second.

Forming the Plan

By this stage of the conference, participants will not generally be thinking about punishment per se, so the conversation should shift to the next steps to restore relationships and make amends. The victim or the representative is asked "What needs to happen now to make things right for you?" and others are also invited to contribute suggestions about what should happen after the conference to restore the situation and relationships. For serious behaviors, it is likely that the offender will be required to accept natural consequences such as in-school suspension for a period of time depending on the nature of the offense. Not all follow-up actions or the details of follow-up need to be determined at the formal conference, however, and the facilitator can guide the group to identify who at the conference will take agency for follow-up regarding specific issues. The school psychologist, for example, is likely to be the person responsible for working with TJ, his teachers, and family members in designing a program to address problems identified at the conference. The principal will be the person responsible for in-school suspension requirements, along with teacher and family input into the contract for in-school suspension. The mathematics teacher might take on responsibility to work with TJ on homework issues. School personnel might be expected to take more agency to follow up with students when there has been a verbal exchange in the classroom, like the one that happened to Sam contributing to violence after school.

Bringing the Conference to a Close

The facilitator calls the conference to a close by highlighting progress made and thanking everyone for their participation. The facilitator should also summarize succinctly the agreed follow-up actions and/or persons responsible for follow-up. This is often the time when statements of reconciliation, regret, or commitment to change might be made by the offender—but this should not be forced as there is little value in encouraging insincerity if such statements come through social pressure and not from the heart. Before participants leave, refreshments should be offered again so that everyone has the opportunity to leave on a social note rather than directly after a 90-minute meeting.

Activity: Read the description of an incident of "Peer Conflict in Elementary School" and review how a formal conference might map the problem and then the solution for Casey and his school.

The Incident: Peer Conflict in Elementary School

Casey: Casey is a 7-year-old boy in second grade at his neighborhood elementary school. He started at this same school in kindergarten and is described as being very bright and performing slightly above average in reading and mathematics. He has always been an extremely active boy, and he had had minor and major difficulties in the past two years including (a) engaging in risky behaviors such as running with scissors, being rough on the playground and in gym, and running through the corridors after waiting until the last minute to transition; (b) bumping, punching, and hitting peers on the playground, seemingly as part of rough play but not tempered until other boys complain; (c) being distracted in the classroom, not paying attention, and poking classmates while they are trying to work; and (d) challenging the teacher when told to get started on his work or to stop bothering others. There were several incidents last year where he was sent to the office, his parents were called, and his behavior would improve slightly for 1 to 2 weeks but nothing seemed to stick.

Background: Casey has not been referred for any special services, and his behavior to date has been viewed as naughty rather than symptomatic of a more serious condition. However, his second grade teacher has discussed Casey's behavior with his parents and also mentioned referring him to the school psychologist because of concern that Casey's problems are escalating. His parents express support for the teacher's efforts to work on Casey's behavior and report that he is hyperactive at home as well. He plays with the same three to four boys regularly, but frequent conflict also characterizes these interactions.

The Incident Report: Casey's class was finishing up an art project that required students to work in groups of four to create a 3-dimensional figure. His group seemed to be having difficulty getting the task done, and the teacher looked up from the other side of the room to see them arguing loudly. He saw Casey push one of the other students, who fell onto the floor. Before the teacher could get to them, one of the other students started shouting at Casey while the fourth student shouted back, defending Casey. The teacher got to the group just as it appeared inevitable that a fight would break out.

IN-SCHOOL SUSPENSION

In any school, suspending a student is a serious issue, and increases in suspensions overall are of concern to everyone. Young people are suspended for behaviors that challenge adults and their schools, and many of these youth also exhibit learning difficulties. Failure to intervene effectively with severe behaviors early can lead to the development of ongoing conduct disorders that become increasingly intractable as the child grows older. Suspension is generally seen as a last resort response that can protect others in the environment from the child's behavior and also communicate a clear message to the child and his or her family that some behavior cannot be tolerated in classrooms and in the school.

Suspension does provide temporary "relief" for schools as well as behavioral consequences for the children involved. Suspension can also remove the risk of harm to other students and to the teacher. However, there are other risks that suspension can create:

- Students sent home from school miss valuable learning opportunities and fall further behind academically.
- Students may be unsupervised or poorly supervised once they leave school, creating the potential for further behavioral difficulties to develop.
- Particularly for teenagers, the suspended student may actually encourage peers to be truant to join him or her while away from school.
- Sending students away from school may actually function as a reward for some children and youth.
- When students are excluded from school, for any reason, this can function as a negative message to them that—whenever the going gets tough—they are in fact not wanted and do not belong in the school community. A metaphor for this would be parents having their child removed from the family based on bad behavior—just as this shouldn't be a consequence at home, it cannot be a consequence at school.
- Families may lack the capacity to provide a structured and constructive environment for them while out of school, hence they may return to school with even more problems following suspension.
- The child's home situation (solo parent, neglectful, or abusive family) might be part of the problem, and the stress on the primary caregiver of having the child at home for a period of time can potentially increase abuse in the family situation.

A Restorative and Educative Approach: In-School Suspension

A restorative approach to serious behavior allows the student to make amends, works to repair damage, and maintains the school's major purpose to be educative by ensuring that the student in suspension does not fall further behind academically while suspended. In-school suspension for severe behavior shifts the ostensible purpose of suspension from punishment (which it often is not) to natural consequences, clearly communicating that behavior is unacceptable in a manner that doesn't introduce further risks but is instead restorative and maintains high expectations for the student (Ministry of Education Special Programs Branch, 1999).

Key principles for in-school suspension consistent with an overall restorative school discipline framework are the following:

- The student remains a valued member of the school community, even while serious consequences are being delivered for unacceptable behavior.
- The student continues to be responsible for learning, and negative behavior does not provide a pathway to avoid school work and completion of curriculum requirements.
- The student will participate in constructive, educative processes toward reshaping more positive behavior as well as continuing to learn throughout disciplinary procedures.
- Both adults and the student engage in a process of restoration and mutual understanding, rather than a process of blame and punishment.
- The school maintains its commitment to every student's full participation in the school community and the learning opportunities it offers.
- Consequences for behavior will not be delivered at the expense of learning and opportunity for positive behavior change.

For in-school suspension to work, it must be one component of a schoolwide comprehensive approach to restorative school discipline. It is not a substitute for an overall commitment to restorative school discipline (Chapter 1); schoolwide behavioral expectations and attention to cultural issues (Chapters 2–3); professional development for staff (Chapter 8); ongoing processes for prevention and intervention (Chapter 3); individualized child-focused intervention services (Chapter 4); and decision making about the seriousness of behavior and the school's response to incidents (Chapter 5). Traditional approaches to children whose relationships have been damaged or broken because of their behavior in an incident causing harm have been to exclude them, with an out-of-school suspension or exclusion consequence operating outside the educational purposes of school and communicating powerful messages about punitive resolution of conflict. Instead, this chapter builds on a metaphorical loop or circle whereby actions taken to resolve conflict must cycle back to the principles and values of peaceful resolution of conflict. Actions taken following conflict must allow participants to be heard, must allow amends to be made, and must not jeopardize any child's safety or educational future. Thus, the process of in-school suspension presented in the next section closes the loop so that schoolwide restorative practices are reflected at all levels of prevention and intervention including how the school responds to the most serious behavior.

It is crucial that in-school suspension functions exactly parallel to how out-of-school suspension previously was used. That is, use of in-school suspension is the consequence for serious behavior incidents (according to processes specified in the school's discipline policy) and cannot be accessed more frequently or for "lesser" behavior *just because the room is there* to avoid addressing behavior management challenges in the classroom. Nor should it be seen as a next-to-final resort whereby out-of-school suspension still operates and hangs as a threat over the heads of adults and children whenever in-school suspension is judged to have not worked.

The message must be clear and unambiguous: Nothing a child does will result in exclusion from school and/or excusing a student from the learning responsibilities. Remember too that in-school suspension *replaces* out-of-school suspension—it is not another tool in the toolbox! From a restorative practices perspective, the only circumstances that can justify removing the child from the school building are (a) if a threat assessment identifies that the child has made a serious substantive threat of violence (see Chapter 5) and/or (b) the child is arrested or imprisoned for a crime.

Key components of in-school suspension

If your school is large enough, you may have the resources and staff allocations needed to set up a dedicated system within your own school. Many schools, however, will not be sufficiently resourced or large enough to sustain an in-school suspension system (and room) alone. Hence, your first step is to review the list below and make a determination as to whether you'll pursue this on your own or form a collaborative system with one to four other schools that are within reasonable driving distances from one another and then form a cross-school planning team along with identifying which school building will house the in-school suspension component. Working across two or more schools will add transportation costs for students, but it will lead to compensating savings in sharing resources and staffing.

Implementing an in-school suspension system in your school involves the following recommended steps:

Step 1: Through discussion with your board, school personnel, and families, reach agreement to trial in-school suspension for a 2-year period, providing 6-monthly reports on its use, effectiveness, and any issues or challenges that arise.

Step 2: Ensure that all school personnel are familiar with the school's behavior expectations, schoolwide discipline policy and restorative justice components, individualized supports for students, and team and network supports for staff.

Step 3: Based on the results of your school's Professional Development Needs Assessment for Restorative Discipline survey, schedule a school-based teacher workshop on restorative classroom discipline. Your district or school-based behavioral specialist support personnel should be able to organize and deliver this session for your teachers.

Step 4: Identify space and furniture for the in-school suspension room—preferably near the school office and not near student traffic areas—and organize funding for a trained paraprofessional to staff the room full-time during school hours including provision for substitute personnel when needed.

Step 5: Working with your behavioral specialist staff, recruit and train the paraprofessional who will staff the room, ensuring that this person is knowledgeable about school procedures (see Step 2 above). Formalize any necessary interagency support agreements and district approvals.

Step 6: Prior to implementation of the in-school suspension process, prepare a written communication describing the rationale and process for distribution to school personnel, students, and families.

Step 7: Develop a full-day's schedule for students in the room that does not align with the general schedule for bathroom breaks, recess, and lunch periods so that there will be no time overlap between suspended students' times out of the room and those of other students at the school, particularly for students in the same age-grade range as those suspended on any given day.

Step 8: Establish a teacher-student in-school suspension contract that includes daily requirements aligned with curriculum activities during the framework of the suspension including homework and any assessments/assignments expected of classmates who are not suspended during that same time frame.

Step 9: Establish a home-school communication template for daily reporting from school to home and from home to school regarding activities in the in-school suspension room and follow-through at home (generally this will be expected homework).

Ongoing: Establish policy and guidelines for operation of the in-school suspension room and process, including completion of the in-school suspension reflections by teacher and student whenever a student is suspended. Sample reflection sheets are provided in Table 11. Guidelines also need to be developed for daily schoolwork assignments for the student from the teacher, regular feedback (at least every 2 days) on work from the teacher to the student, how the family will be involved and kept informed, and a restorative conference process for returning to the classroom at the end of the suspension period.

Table 11   Sample Reflection Sheets for Students and Teachers

---

In-School Suspension Reflections

Student Reflection   Name: _____

                                     Teacher/staff name:_____

The purpose behind this sheet is to help you think about what happened, why, and where to go from here. It is not about blame and punishment but is about working things out for the better. This sheet will be seen by the teacher and the consultant.

Please answer the questions honestly and clearly.

1. Do you think it was fair that you were sent to in-school suspension? Why?

2. What were you doing when you were sent?

3. What were you thinking or feeling when you were sent?

(Continued)

(Continued)

---

4. Did your behavior affect other students? How?

5. What could you have done differently so that you could stay in class?

6. What things need to change for you to return to class?

Please leave this with the in-school suspension teacher.

Staff In-School Suspension Reflection Name: _____

Student name: _____

The purpose behind this sheet is to reflect on what happened, why, and where to from here. It is not about blame and punishment but is about working things out for the better. The student will have a similar sheet to complete.

1. What was the student's behavior that resulted in being sent to in-school suspension?

2. What interventions had you done before sending the student to in-school suspension?

3. Were other students affected by the behavior? Who was affected and how?

4. What could you have done differently that may have resulted in the student modifying his/her behavior?

5. How could you change classroom practices in the future to manage this student's behavior?

6. What happens next with this student?

Please keep this sheet, as it will be useful as part of the working-through process. You may wish to discuss it with the principal, dean, or head of department.

Source: Adapted from procedures used at a New Zealand high school, Paeora College, 2008.

Organizing space, staff, and scheduling for in-school suspension

Three critical and obvious requirements for an effective in-school suspension program are space, staff, and scheduling (Steps 4, 5, and 7). You'll need a designated and dedicated room for in-school suspension that may not have any students using the room on any given day but which is available continuously whenever it is needed. You'll also need a staff member who has the appropriate training and background to staff the room, and this person—like the room—must be available daily and on a moment's notice whenever there is need for in-school suspension. This staffing will also require backup staff, which can generally be someone else at the school who may have other duties (hence does not need to be available unless the regular in-school staff person is absent) but can be reassigned should a replacement be needed.

The in-school suspension room

An in-school suspension room must be located away from general student areas and preferably near the office complex. It should be large enough to accommodate furniture, the staff member, and up to an estimated maximum number of students likely to be suspended at any given time, which you can determine based on previous out-of-school suspension figures (plus one).

Location. The room should not be near classrooms or other general student areas. To the maximum extent possible, its location should preclude contact with or visibility to other students. This physical separation will not only be reassuring to other students and their families where suspension was for incidents involving safety; it also prevents the possibility that the suspended student could show off or behave in such as way that he'll be regarded as an antihero by peers.

Figure 3 In-School Suspension Room

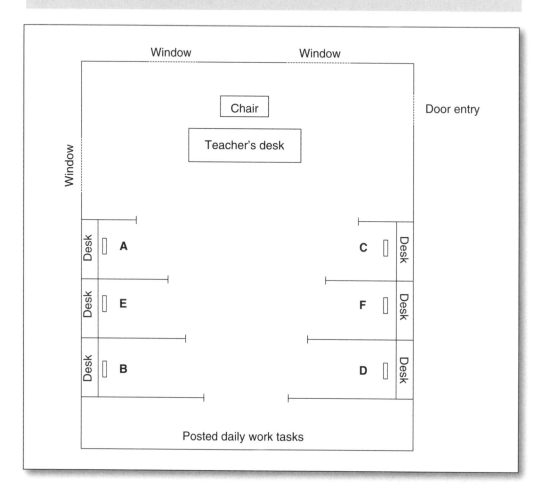

Ideally, this room should be within the administrative complex of the school, which generally ensures a separate entrance off the main entry, more private transitions, proximity to a restroom for toilet breaks, and access to main office personnel including the principal in case of emergency.

Physical Characteristics of the Room. For most schools, the room will need to be approximately half the size of a typical classroom and should look much like a small classroom. It should not resemble a time-out room in size or shape, and it should not have the feel of a punishment or depressing area. After all, the staff member as well as the student will be spending the entire day in this room, so having windows is important!

The room will require a teacher's desk and several student work stations. The teacher's desk must be positioned so that students seated at any of the work stations in the room are visible to the staff member who, if seated at the desk, must be facing the students, have the entry door in line of sight as well, and be able to reach any individual student quickly. Figure 3 illustrates what this arrangement would look like for a room accommodating up to six students at one time.

As can be seen from the diagram, the side partitions for each carrel vary in length to the center of the room so as to ensure that the supervising staff member can see each student seated at his or her desk, but so that the students cannot see one another.

Furniture. Student work stations or carrels comprise a student desk (extending across both sides of the carrel and fixed to the wall at the back), a chair with fixed (not wheeled) legs, the room wall facing the student at the back of the desk, and partitions on two sides of the work station deep enough so that the student seated at the desk will be situated within both sides of the carrel and not visible to students in other carrels. Partitions should be fixed to the floor so that they cannot be moved by students, and they must be approximately 5 feet high.

Seating Arrangements for Students. Students would be assigned individual carrel spaces and desks according to the alphabetical sequence indicated. The purpose would be to achieve maximum separation of the students, so one student would be in the *A* carrel, a second student would then be assigned the *B* carrel, a third student the *C* carrel, and so on.

The in-school suspension staff

A major requirement to operate a successful in-school suspension program is the availability of a trained staff member who must be available to staff the room at all times whenever there is a student assigned to in-school suspension. As there will be days when no students are suspended, this staff person can be a resource to support other school needs on those occasions. However, the individual cannot be permanently or even reliably assigned to other duties given that an incident could occur at any time that would require staff for the in-school suspension room.

Assignment to the room requires that formal processes have been completed with contractual agreements in place for the student's time assigned to in-school suspension. Typically, when an incident occurs that leads to out-of-school suspension, the school will call the student's parents to retrieve the student from school immediately pending completion of formal procedures. With the availability of a dedicated room and staff, the parents would still be called immediately to inform them of the incident and plans for suspension, but the student can be immediately removed to the in-school suspension room. It is useful to have a very clear statement for the parents or caregiver regarding the implications of the suspension. In the traditional model, parents have a variety of reactions. Some, frustrated by the inconvenience of having to leave work and come to fetch their child, can take out their hostility by being unnecessarily punitive and adding a level of punishment at home. However, others will simply blame the school for lack of ability to manage their child's behavior and thus imply to the student that the punishment is unfair. Even more common is the fact that, with very challenging young people, the family situation is quite likely to be highly dysfunctional so that there may be no parental monitoring at all, rendering the suspension essentially meaningless. To obtain the constructive support of parents for the in-school suspension action, it is crucial that time is spent talking to the primary caregiver and explaining what might be expected of them. This, of course, is one of the benefits and goals of the restorative group process.

The trained staff person will need to be available on a moment's notice. In-school suspension does not require a registered teacher, as the student's work while assigned to the room will continue to be the responsibility of his or her teacher(s). However, the staff member should be a qualified paraprofessional who has completed required behavior training in order to carry out the responsibilities associated with the program. We recommend that this person be someone who has already had some experience working in a school within that particular community (e.g., as a teacher aid, bus driver, playground supervisor, etc.) but not necessarily any formal training as a teacher. Preferably, the person should be someone who can interact positively with students for the age range in the school, has the personal disposition to have a neutral affect with high expectations for student work, completes specified behavior training, and passes a police check. Selecting someone who also matches the cultural and/or language background of any minoritized student cultural or ethnic groups that tend to be overrepresented in the school's disciplinary statistics would be ideal.

The in-school suspension schedule

Put in place a daily schedule for the student during time spent in in-school suspension. One logistical reason for the schedule is to ensure that meal and break or recess times do not overlap with those of the classes from which the student has been suspended. To the maximum extent possible, there is to be no social contact between the suspended student and the peers or other adults with the exception of the teacher who is involved in providing work and giving the student feedback on that work. The substantive reason for having a definite schedule is to communicate to the student that school days continue to be work days with set time periods to complete work—being in the room should not establish poor work habits nor communicate to the student that he or she is driving what happens when. The daily schedule should represent time allocated to different subjects working on assignments provided to the in-school suspension supervisor by the teacher or teachers involved with the student's program.

Teachers will be providing sufficient materials so that the student spends approximately the same amount of time on the work in each area as are his or her same-age peers in the regular classroom. Time should also be allocated for regular feedback to the student on completed work from the classroom teacher, who should come to the room to meet with the student at least (certainly no less than) every 2 to 3 days. Finally, the student should arrive and depart from the in-school suspension room on a different timetable from the same-age peers, perhaps either 5 to 10 minutes earlier or 5 to 10 minutes later than other students.

The student–teacher contract and home–school communications

Another important feature of in-school suspension is communications with the home. In-school suspension is a serious consequence signaled by a serious incident, and it is crucial that the student's family be involved in the restoration process. At the time that the suspension period is set, agreement should be reached about the schedule of communications with the home: we recommend that there be contact between the in-school suspension staff member and the home for every 2 to 3 days of suspension to report on how things are going, and that the student's classroom teacher talk with the parents at least once every 5 days during the suspension period. We suggest that a formal contract statement be signed by the parents, the student, and relevant school personnel (see the model contract form in Table 12).

Table 12   The Home–School In-School Suspension Contract

Description of the incident leading to in-school suspension:

Date/time of the restorative school conference:

Location of the conference:

Who from the family (and relationship) will be attending:

(Continued)

(Continued)

Contract

The principal or his/her representative has discussed with me the incident resulting in in-school suspension and procedures required for restoration and restitution. I understand that my son/daughter will be required to keep up to date with his/her schoolwork during the time spent in in-school suspension, and I agree to support him/her in this process including supervision of homework. Further, I agree to participate in regular communication as described below with both the staff supervisor of the in-school suspension room and the teacher who is named below. My son/daughter has also signed below to indicate his/her acceptance of these terms.

Parent Signature: Date:

Student Signature: Date:

Staff Supervisor Signature: Date:

Classroom Teacher Signature: Date:

Principal Signature: Date:

Communication process (describe briefly):

SUMMARY

This chapter provides detailed descriptions of tertiary intervention procedures that will be handled by school leaders at school level—the formal restorative school conference and a model for in-school suspension. These two components of restorative school discipline ensure that there are appropriate consequences that are nevertheless restorative for serious behavior. Follow-up to behavioral incidents that can and do cause harm must ensure safety for all participants without jeopardizing or compromising the restorative ethos of the school and inclusion of all its students. Both a well-established system of restorative conferencing and the provision for in-school suspension are consistent with the values of restorative school discipline while protecting everyone involved.

The difference between these concepts and a more traditional disciplinary approach is that the latter is heavily dependent on negative consequences for inappropriate behavior. But punishment is notoriously ineffectual as a way of changing behavior, unless it is quite severe and immediate, and that is rarely possible or practical for an organization such as a school, even if it were ethical and humane. Harsh punishments elicit emotional responses from the people being punished, even if deep down they recognize that it was justified. Students who feel disrespected, treated differently from other more favored students, or humiliated in front of their peers will feel anger and think of ways of retaliating against authority. And neither is the threat of punishment an effective motivator of positive, prosocial behavior.

At the end of the day, schools do not have a great degree of control over students who are determined to be as difficult and confrontational as they can be. Unless students see the importance of an education, enjoy their school experience, feel valued by teachers, have positive peer relationships, and are committed to fitting in with the expected standards of decorum, the management of behavior with strategies such as time out, criticism, loss of privileges, detention, and suspension will simply not be effective. The procedures explained in this chapter provide a fundamentally different model for managing behavior, but one that recognizes the seriousness of many student actions and the importance of responding to them in a calculatingly firm and consistent manner.

Section III
Evaluating Outcomes and Sustainability

7 Evaluating Student Outcomes

This chapter describes processes for school use to evaluate the effectiveness of interventions for individual children and schoolwide restorative practices. Individual school districts are likely to have requirements in place to monitor student achievement, and these would apply to students with behavioral challenges as they do for any student. In addition, there may be child development or behavioral measures that have been individually selected based on the student's diagnosis or developmental repertoire. Regardless of the requirements of your school or district, you as school leader will want some assurances that the time and effort toward implementation of a particular intervention approach is time well spent. The measures included in this chapter are designed to enable you to make such judgments toward determining whether a program is working well or alternatives are needed.

MEANINGFUL OUTCOMES FOR STUDENTS AND SCHOOLS

Policies and practices have impact on students, school personnel, overall school climate, families, and the school community. Even where it is difficult to assert a causal effect, changes that parallel the implementation of particular strategies suggest a direct relationship. Of course, interventions should result in meaningful outcomes, and we expect positive changes to be occurring as a consequence of planned interventions and school activities. There can also be unplanned negative changes that are so closely aligned with the implementation of a new strategy that the possibility of negative side effects must also be carefully considered.

The design and implementation of schoolwide and child-focused interventions and activities involve time, effort, and resources. Hence, it is crucial that evaluation activities are part of the planning so that everyone can have confidence that the program is in fact resulting in the intended positive outcomes and not producing unintended negative side effects. Without proper evaluation, children's precious time may be lost as already negative patterns become even more entrenched and difficult to change. Furthermore, personnel time and school resources that could make a difference are wasted. Having a clear evaluation plan is essential, and it doesn't have to be complicated. In this chapter, we outline a series of user-friendly tools that can be used to monitor the effectiveness of behavioral interventions. These tools have high utility for use by busy professionals in settings where multiple demands do not allow the kinds of clinical precision that might be reported in the published literature or in private practice with unlimited resources. The validity of user-friendly tools has been established, and they can provide information that is more useful to educators and families than more elegant measures accompanied by detailed reports (Meyer & Janney, 1989).

Overall Developmental Measures

The first outcome measure that should be firmly in place anytime individual children are receiving specialized services is a measure of child development and behavior change that is administered at least annually. Whenever individualized services are provided to students on the assumption that those services will have beneficial outcomes, there should be evidence that this is so. Measurement of child change over time should entail use of agreed, psychometrically validated measures for which norms exist or are being established in a way that is appropriate for the cultural groups served by the school. Normative data tell us the level of change expected through maturation alone, so we can assess how a particular child is doing in relationship to age norms.

For students with developmental disabilities, for example, a measure such as the Scales of Independent Behavior (SIB) can be most helpful as it is well standardized internationally, including 14 adaptive behavior scales and eight scales representing problem behavior (Bruininks, Woodcock, Weatherman, & Hill, 1996). For students who are diagnosed as having conduct disorders, measures such as the Strengths and Difficulties Questionnaire (Goodman, 1997), the Social Skills Rating System (Gresham & Elliott, 1990), and the Child Behavior Checklist (Achenbach, 1991) are commonly used to reveal whether behavior is improving over time as a function of the intervention program. These measures require administration by someone with the appropriate qualifications such as a licensed psychologist (or mental health specialist), services generally available depending on student referral and eligibility for special education and mental health services.

Meaningful Behavior Change

Each of the following changes in a student's behavior is important in determining whether a particular intervention is effective:

- The problem behavior improves (the challenging behavior is no longer a problem or has decreased and become more easily managed).
- Replacement skills are acquired (the student is using new skills that have been taught in situations that previously resulted in behavior problems).
- New metacognitive skills are being used to manage behavior (the student has gained insight and control over his or her own behavior, predicting and preventing outbursts, etc. by using positive thinking strategies).
- There are positive collateral effects and no negative side effects (rather than a new behavior problem occurring, the student is generally doing well and relating well with others).
- The student's placement and daily schedule is normalized (rather than requiring in-school suspension, special seating arrangements, etc., the student seems fine following the same routines as his or her age peers).
- Both the student and significant others are pleased with the results (whereas previously both the student and those in the environment felt stressed by interactions, there now seems to be a fit with positive relationships developing).

We would argue that the further down the above list one goes, the more meaningful the outcomes. Thus, if the child, the family, and the teacher are pleased with how things are going, this is far more meaningful than detailed checklists or charts of the frequency or intensity of individual problem behaviors. Further, an intervention cannot really be phased out or considered to be successful unless and until the people involved are satisfied with the outcome and the student has learned new skills and developed new, positive relationships—no matter what a checklist says. Similarly, if the student is still subjected to highly restrictive and controlling circumstances rather than participating fully in typical, age-appropriate activities, we don't really know if improvements in behavior have any relevance to real life.

USER-FRIENDLY DATA COLLECTION

A comprehensive and useful view of data collection goes beyond measuring problem behavior incidents and incorporates other evidence of the direct and indirect effects of that behavior. Evidence that an intervention has had a positive impact can include the following:

1. *New skills*: Rather than becoming angry and lashing out at others when frustrated or provoked, the student has learned how to ask for help or excuse himself or herself from uncomfortable situations in socially acceptable ways in order to recover composure.

2. *Behavior problems*: The problem behavior either isn't occurring at all or is occurring so seldom that both teachers and parents feel it is not really a problem any longer.

3. *Daily schedule and tasks*: Whereas previously the student was able to stay on task for only some of the time and tasks were modified, he or she is now able to follow the same schedule as the other students in the classroom.

4. *Daily log success ratings*: The teacher reports that a typical day with the student is now going well. In addition, the kinds of activities that used to provoke problem behavior no longer do so, and the student is now successful in typical classroom activities and tasks working alongside others.

5. *Disciplinary actions*: School records show a decline in the number of referrals for suspensions and exclusions, and individual students who were previously referred often are no longer being referred.

6. *Incident records*: A comparison of office referrals and reports of incidents requiring action shows improvements both in the frequency and seriousness of challenging behavior such as aggression and disruption.

Many of the above outcomes can be monitored through data already required in schools (e.g., office referrals, suspensions, placement records, student schedules, incident records), and others can be recorded periodically by staff rather than requiring intensive and direct behavior observation and recording (e.g., daily logs, teacher ratings of student success). School personnel are sometimes asked to keep continuous data collection records such as checking for the presence or absence of a problem behavior every 15 minutes during selected time periods or recording frequencies across the day. While such intensive data collection systems can provide accurate information about behavior over time, it is difficult to envision how a busy regular classroom teacher with responsibility for 25 to 35 students could do this for one student. Consequently, such data collection systems are more likely to be found in special education classrooms or by the use of supplementary personnel such as a teacher aid (or a graduate student doing research). Even in specialist settings, however, it may not be feasible to keep accurate and reliable data on individual target behaviors without additional staff to do so. Fortunately, the kinds of alternatives described in these guides that fit more easily into busy schools and classrooms can provide information that is just as useful for evaluating the effectiveness of interventions.

DATA COLLECTION FOR PROBLEM BEHAVIOR

There are various data collection approaches to monitoring instances of problem behavior that is the focus of an individualize intervention plan. Most require that a record be kept by a teacher or other staff member, but some may actually be recorded by the student. The guides highlight several approaches that have demonstrated validity, are user-friendly for busy people, and can also provide valuable information to inform the intervention plan.

Self-Monitoring

Your school consultant may recommend that the student himself or herself keep data on behaviors that are problematic. A student may, for example, keep an *anger log* to record agreed instances where something happens that has typically resulted in problem behavior such as aggression or defiance. Self-recording contributes to the intervention in making the student more aware of the kinds of incidents that are problematic, requiring reflection on the incident as well as reporting on what happened next. The student typically shares the log with the school psychologist, and they work together to problem-solve future situations. An additional advantage of self-recording systems such as an anger log is that the log also provides a record that can be examined for improvements over time. As part of this process, the school psychologist has a running record—at least from the student's point of view—of the student's anger management over time.

Daily Log

A *daily log* can also be kept to record the student's behavior and thus provide a record of how the teacher views the behavior over the same time frame (see Figure 4). The daily log doesn't actually have to be completed every day but could be done twice weekly on a predetermined schedule, such as marking in advance 2 random days each week on a calendar for an upcoming 4-week period (it is important to keep filling out the log on the agreed randomly selected dates rather than targeting good or bad days). The teacher would agree to spend 10 minutes at the end of those 2 days each week filling in the log. Within 3 to 4 weeks, there will be a significant amount of information about the student that not only provides evidence about whether the intervention is working but also can be used to problem-solve making things better. A daily log can also help caregivers to see patterns that might not otherwise have been noticed but also are clearly having an impact on behavior—it may even reveal ways in which the mediators (teacher, teacher aid, parent) completing the log should change their own behavior to provide more support to the student.

Figure 4 Sample Daily Log

DAILY LOG

Student's name:_____ Date/Day of week:_____

Log entry by:_____

1. Overall, what kind of day did the student have?(circle one number only)

1	2	3	4	5
Very good day	Okay	Not sure	Not okay	Very bad day

2. How well did the student do on tasks and activities today?(circle one number only)

1	2	3	4	5
Very good day	Okay	Not sure	Not okay	Very bad day

3. How well did the student get on with other students today?(circle one number only)

1	2	3	4	5
Very well	Okay	Not sure	Not okay	Very badly

- Comment briefly on the day's events and the student's behavior. Note any incidents that occurred that seem important to you (positive and negative).
- Tasks/activities the student especially enjoyed and/or worked well on
- Tasks/activities the student did not enjoy and/or work well on

Source: Adapted from Meyer and Janney (1989).

Narrative daily logs such as these are actually quite good at helping caregivers learn more about the student—which is directly relevant to the student's capacity to improve. By reporting how the students perform on tasks that they do or do not enjoy, patterns will also emerge that can provide useful information in program planning. The teacher judgment ratings on a scale of 1 to 5 may seem arbitrary, but in fact, it is the teacher's perceptions about the student that do define success on the task. Best of all, the daily log is not onerous, thus it is far more likely to actually get done in comparison to a complex, demanding data collection record.

Daily and Weekly Schedules

A weekly schedule of the student's activities in a particular class or classroom can provide a great deal of useful information if it is completed once at referral, periodically during an intervention phase (perhaps 3 to 4 times in all across 2 to 3 months), and then again when the school psychologist feels the program has run its course. Figure 5 shows a sample schedule that the teacher would complete for a given student, recording the nature of student activities and grouping arrangements along with teacher comments and a rating regarding how well things progressed. By comparing these entries for different activities and grouping configurations, it might become evident that a particular student is doing well controlling problem behavior in whole class instruction and independent seatwork but having difficulty in small group work. The school intervention team can then engage the student in the problem-solving process about how to address remaining challenges. Again, this is the kind of data collection device that does not require an inordinate amount of time and has the advantage of providing information to monitor effects and also contribute to improving the intervention.

A successful intervention will show observable ecological and daily schedule changes that are age appropriate. Ratings by key caregivers will also become increasingly positive. Given that these caregivers are in fact the mediators interacting with the student in the school and classroom, their satisfaction and perceptions about the student's behavior are valid indicators of whether or not the behavior is improving.

Incident Records

Schools are required to record serious incidents whenever extreme reactive strategies were needed and used (e.g., crisis management for aggression). These incident records are intended to ensure that rights are protected and to provide evidence that the school took appropriate

Figure 5 Sample Student Schedule Record

Child's Weekly Schedule

Date	Activity	Time	Grouping [a]	Staff	Rating [b]	Comments

Date	Activity	Time	Grouping	Staff	Rating	Comments

Source: Adapted from Meyer and Janney (1989).

a. Grouping arrangement code: 1:1 = One-to-one instruction; I = Independent; P = Pairs; G = Small group; C = Whole class.

b. Rating code: + = Went well, successful; V = Varied; O = Not successful.

measures to ensure safety for everyone concerned. The very same *incident record* can be adapted to provide an evidence base for individual changes in student behavior as well as school rates of problem behavior across time to evaluate the impact of policy changes. The sample incident record in Figure 6 does more than record what happened in requiring more detail surrounding the incident. The record would then provide additional information that can be used by the school principal and the team as part of their planning for future interventions.

Figure 6 Sample Incident Record

Incident Record

Completed by: _____

Child's name: _____   Activity taking place: _____

Where: _____   Date/Day of week: _____   Time: _____

Staff present when incident occurred: _____

Children present when incident occurred: _____

_____

1. Describe what happened just before behavior occurred. For example, was the child prompted? Was a staff person attending to the child? Was the child alone?

2. Describe what the child did and what happened through the incident. For example, how intense was the behavior? How long did it last?

3. Describe what happened to the child immediately after the incident: Include any consequences deliberately applied and also those that occurred without planning. For example, did other adults and/or children gather around? Did task demands stop? Did adults and/or children who were present get excited or stay calm?

4. Why do you think the incident occurred?

5. How do you think the behavior could have been prevented or handled differently?

Source: Adapted from Meyer and Evans (1989).

An incident record such as this is completed immediately after a serious incident by the person who managed the student during the incident. It incorporates descriptive information (date/time, situation, who was present, what happened, intensity/duration, how it was managed) and reflections (why it occurred, how it might have been prevented). Reflections may not be accurate, but knowing how mediators view an incident and what they think is going on can be most helpful to intervention planning, and encouraging staff to reflect can also reveal insights and good ideas. The more generic, schoolwide incident record in Chapter 5 sits alongside the more individualized incident record represented in Figure 6. Taken together, these two records can provide the principal with valuable information and insight regarding challenges and opportunities to address those challenges.

SUMMARY

Overarching school discipline policies and practices are designed to have a positive impact on student behavior and learning. Similarly, today's educational systems provide intensive intervention services, supports, and programs to meet the needs of individual students with behavioral challenges. To determine whether or not these approaches are having the desired impact and effects on students and the school community, the principal will want to have a set of evaluation measures or tools that can and will be implemented alongside interventions. In our experience, these measures can be user-friendly and, at the same time, actually provide far more useful information for schools than traditional behavioral monitoring observation systems or checklists. User-friendly measures have the added advantage of being well suited for use by busy professionals. Many of them can also be adapted easily for use by parents and the students themselves, offering the opportunity to gain insight into behavior, thus going beyond simply monitoring behavior. The most important issue is whether data collection will be done, so making it simple and useful helps to ensure that this happens. We end with a paraphrased quote that says it well:

Don't ruin good with perfect!

8 Professional Learning for Sustainability

Meaningful implementation of restorative school discipline cannot occur unless school personnel have essential knowledge, skills, and understandings about restorative practices. One of the responsibilities of the school leader is to ensure that staff are professionally prepared for restorative approaches to school discipline and school safety. Particularly as these are areas of rapid development, the principal should have in place a system for annual assessment of staff capabilities. This chapter provides an overview of key competencies needed for restorative school discipline and a mechanism for annual staff needs assessment to drive professional development priorities and activities at the school. It includes the Professional Development (PD) Needs Assessment for Restorative Discipline for use by the principal with school personnel.

THE NEED FOR ONGOING PROFESSIONAL DEVELOPMENT

School leaders are responsible for and work with a diverse teaching and support staff. Restorative school discipline works well when supported by a strong foundation of policy and practices that are well understood and agreed by all school personnel—who have the knowledge to implement practices with integrity. It is tempting to assume that teachers already know about classroom management and that all teachers are committed to supporting learning and inclusion for all students. But just as the student population has become increasingly diverse, the teaching population also varies and represents different background experiences and expertise. At any school, there will be teachers who have been at that particular school for many years, teachers who are recently graduated and new to teaching, and experienced teachers who have come from another school or even another geographic region including from another country.

Restorative school discipline approaches conflict in a fundamentally different way with the usual approaches to dealing with offenses that characterizes our traditional legal system. Most adults have basic experience with positive rewards for good behavior and retributive punishment for transgressions and accept these as the norm. Teachers who have well-grounded pedagogical and classroom management competencies will have mastered the skill set of being *warm demanders.* Kleinfeld (1975) first used this term to refer to having high expectations for Native Alaskan and Native American students that were expressed through caring and warm relationships rather than through authoritative directives and demands. The concept has since been elaborated further as particularly important for many other cultural groups as well by Ross, Bondy, Gallingane, and Hambacher (2008) and Ware (2006). Teachers who are warm demanders seem naturally able to bring out the best in their students, though even skillful teachers will experience difficulties knowing how to react when a student doesn't respond to a classroom context that seems to be working well for nearly everyone else.

Some teachers may take for granted that their students know what is expected of them in the classroom and may initially be unwilling or unable to deal with students who seem resistant to meeting those expectations. Teaching and learning activities in classrooms have historically been teacher centered, with the teacher as the central source of authority driving the agenda for learning. More contemporary approaches to pedagogy in the classroom emphasize the importance of more discursive and student-centered teaching and learning that involve students actively in contributing to their own learning rather than passively responding to teachers. Discursive strategies have also been demonstrated to have the capacity to be more culturally responsive to students from diverse cultural and linguistic backgrounds (Hynds et al., 2011; Savage et al., 2011; Sleeter, 2011). Teachers who are very directive rather than discursive in their approach to pedagogy may not be accustomed to involving the children themselves in setting rules for classroom behavior. Interestingly, Savage and her colleagues found that the more traditional teachers using primarily teacher-directed approaches struggled most with classroom management.

Teachers may also consider that it is not their job to handle students whose behavior falls outside what they consider reasonable or safe—expecting someone else such as special education personnel or you as the principal to solve serious behavior problems. Even today, many teachers may have limited knowledge of different cultural perspectives and will have varied views about whether the school should fit the child or the child should fit the school (Sleeter, 2011). In secondary schools in particular, a proportion of the teaching staff may feel strongly that teachers are there to teach the subject and that the child's socioemotional life is not their business. It is also the case that even teachers who are willing in principle to be inclusive may nevertheless lack practical strategies to diffuse difficult situations in classrooms. Without professional development, they are likely to be unable to respond constructively to children who exhibit serious behavior that could put themselves and others at risk for harm.

It is very helpful for school leaders to be knowledgeable about what school personnel know and believe about the innovative principles and ideas promoted in the school and wider educational community. Not every teacher will be au fait with the concepts of classroom and school restorative discipline, culturally responsive practices, socioemotional support, and high expectations for learning and behavior. You will have information in some areas for personnel who have long been part of your school, but there will be other staff about whom you have less information. There will also be particular topical areas where most staff may have had little formal training, such as culturally responsive pedagogies applied to different subject areas.

School leaders already engage in various staff appraisal activities that provide a picture of the professional development needs in one's school. Decisions are also made regularly at school and at district level about professional development priorities that will be addressed through special PD initiatives and activities for staff whose participation may be voluntary, negotiated as part of collective bargaining, or compulsory. Thus, the PD issues identified in this chapter related to restorative school discipline are expected only to complement or supplement ongoing PD projects.

THE PD NEEDS-ASSESSMENT TOOL FOR RESTORATIVE DISCIPLINE

Rather than making assumptions about where your school staff are at or what they already know, we recommend use of a more systematic needs assessment to prioritize PD activities and opportunities. While the principal cannot be fully responsible for everything that individual teachers and other school personnel know and do, we advocate that school leaders must *assume agency* for having a positive influence on professional development that is based, as much as possible, on sound information rather than assumptions or conjecture. Taking agency is a slightly different concept than admonitions that educators should take or accept responsibility for something. Taking agency recognizes that the educator *can* make a difference hence becomes agentic in doing so. Taking or accepting responsibility has a more negative connotation in suggesting active refusal to do so, when the real issue might rather be that there is a lack of knowledge of what to do.

To assist school leaders in identifying exactly what the challenges are, a sample needs assessment is included at the end of this chapter in order to help in this process of prioritizing planned professional development activities for the upcoming year and annually thereafter. The PD Needs Assessment for Restorative Discipline may be completed by the school's senior management team (including heads of departments in high schools) and/or adapted for completion by school personnel as part of their self-planning for teacher PD. This PD needs assessment tool includes questions about all relevant components and input into determining priorities for PD opportunities. We recognize that the person completing the needs assessment won't always know what he or she doesn't know, and school leaders are unlikely to know what the teachers and other school personnel in their schools know. But having staff review the list of terms and concepts included in the needs assessment will provide opportunity to begin the process of acknowledging where there are gaps and where improvements can be made in professional skills and understandings.

THE PD NEEDS ASSESSMENT FOR RESTORATIVE DISCIPLINE

Rate your *best estimate* of the extent to which teachers and other school personnel at your school can demonstrate each of the following:

0 = Don't know

1 = None

2 = Some

3 = Most

4 = All

A. Discursive and Culturally Responsive Pedagogy and Classroom Management					
	Don't know	*None*	*Some*	*Most*	*All*
1. Teachers use varied instructional approaches ranging from direct to discursive.	0	1	2	3	4
2. Teachers establish class rules and expectations with student input.	0	1	2	3	4
3. Teachers have knowledge of child development issues and expectations across the age range taught including transition planning.	0	1	2	3	4
4. Teachers are knowledgeable about cooperative learning and use this approach regularly.	0	1	2	3	4
5. Teachers use systematic strategies for organizing students into small groups for in-class learning activities that are based on theories of peer relationships and support networks.	0	1	2	3	4
6. Teachers are skilful in and regularly use classroom conferencing processes for decision making and problem solving.	0	1	2	3	4
7. Teachers use warm demander approaches to support positive behavior for learning in the classroom.	0	1	2	3	4
8. Teachers are knowledgeable about the cultural values and mores of major cultural groups represented in their classrooms and across the school.	0	1	2	3	4
9. Teachers incorporate at least some linguistic and cultural knowledge and icons into their classroom activities for nondominant cultural student groups represented in the school population.	0	1	2	3	4
10. Teachers have well-developed practices for positive and ongoing home-school communications involving their students.	0	1	2	3	4

(Continued)

(Continued)

	Don't know	None	Some	Most	All
11. Teachers assume agency for participation in annual professional development to enhance their pedagogical and classroom management practices that are evidence based.	0	1	2	3	4
B. Prevention of and Intervention With Behavior Challenges					
	Don't know	*None*	*Some*	*Most*	*All*
12. School personnel understand risks and pathways for children who exhibit behavioral challenges and/or with special needs.	0	1	2	3	4
13. School personnel have basic skills in functional assessment to analyze children's behavioral challenges and problem-solve interventions.	0	1	2	3	4
14. School personnel appreciate that there will be different perspectives on behavior held by diverse cultures represented in the student population and school community, even if they don't know what they are.	0	1	2	3	4
15. School personnel use available referral, support networks, and resources where appropriate to address student needs and challenges.	0	1	2	3	4
16. School personnel have knowledge of the four major components of a positive and educative program to intervene with challenging behavior that can be implemented in typical classroom, school, and community environments.	0	1	2	3	4
17. School personnel understand the important role of mediators in children's lives and can describe processes for *affective priming* to ensure that children have support to acquire new positive behaviors.	0	1	2	3	4
18. Teachers can work collaboratively with consultant expertise to plan, implement, and evaluate an intervention for an individual student with behavioral challenges.	0	1	2	3	4

19. Teachers can work collaboratively with other school personnel to participate actively and constructively in restorative school conferences to address serious behavior challenges and conflict.	0	1	2	3	4
20. Teachers are familiar with the school's in-school suspension policy and practices and understand the process of in-school suspension reflections including how to complete the staff reflection form.	0	1	2	3	4

C. School Safety and Restorative School Discipline Policy

	Don't know	None	Some	Most	All
21. School personnel can list, define, and give examples of five key principles for restorative practices in schools—interpersonal relationships, personal dignity, mutual respect and understanding, restorative conferencing, and restitution.	0	1	2	3	4
22. School personnel are familiar with the questions for a generative restorative script in restorative conferencing.	0	1	2	3	4
23. School personnel have knowledge of reasonable expectations for children's socioemotional capacities at different ages.	0	1	2	3	4
24. School personnel are knowledgeable about minor and major behaviors that require an office discipline referral.	0	1	2	3	4
25. School personnel have basic skills in threat assessment and the actions required depending on the nature of the threat.	0	1	2	3	4
26. School personnel can manage an assault and break up a fight either directly or by contacting the appropriate adult in the school who can intervene immediately.	0	1	2	3	4
27. School personnel are familiar with the school's standard emergency response procedures to ensure school safety and regularly practice relevant components.	0	1	2	3	4

(Continued)

(Continued)

28. School personnel can informally assess a suicide risk and notify the appropriate persons as needed.	0	1	2	3	4
29. School personnel acknowledge bullying and can describe processes for addressing bullying including seeking further advice and support to intervene.	0	1	2	3	4
30. School personnel have knowledge of the policy and practice of restorative school conferencing at the school.	0	1	2	3	4
31. School personnel have knowledge of the policy and practice of in-school suspension at the school.	0	1	2	3	4

References

Achenbach, T. M. (1991). *Manual for the Child Behavior Checklist/4–18 and 1991 Profile.* Burlington: University of Vermont Department of Psychiatry.

Algozzine, B., Daunic, A. P., & Smith, S. W. (2010). *Preventing problem behaviors: Schoolwide programs and classroom practices* (2nd ed.). Thousand Oaks, CA: Corwin.

American Psychological Association. (2004). Warning signs of youth violence. Retrieved from http://www.apahelpcenter.org/featuredtopics/feature.php?id=38&ch=8

American Psychological Association Zero Tolerance Task Force. (2006). *Are zero tolerance policies effective in the schools? An evidentiary review and recommendations.* Washington, DC: American Psychological Association.

Bateman, S., & Berryman, M. (2008). He Hui Whakatika: Culturally responsive, self-determining interventions for restoring harmony. *Kairaranga, 9(1),* 6–11.

Bauer, N. S., Lozano, P., & Rivara, F. P. (2007). The effectiveness of the Olweus Bullying Prevention Program in public middle schools: A controlled trial. *Journal of Adolescent Health, 40,* 266–274.

Bishop, R., & Berryman, M. (2006). *Culture speaks: Cultural relationships and classroom learning.* Wellington, New Zealand: Huia Press.

Blake, C., Wang, W., Cartledge, G., & Gardner, R. (2000). Middle school students with serious emotional disturbances serve as social skills trainers and reinforcers for peers with SED. *Behavioral Disorders, 25,* 280–298.

Brock, S. E. (2002). School suicide postvention. In G. G. Bear, K. M. Minke, & A. Thomas (Eds.), *Children's needs II: Development, problems and alternatives* (pp. 553–576). Bethesda, MD: National Association of School Psychologists.

Brock, S. E., & Sandoval, J. (1997). Suicidal ideation and behaviors. In G. G. Bear, K. M. Minke, & A. Thomas (Eds.), *Children's needs II: Development, problems and alternatives* (pp. 361–374). Bethesda, MD: National Association of School Psychologists.

Bruininks, R. H., Woodcock, R. W., Weatherman, R. F., & Hill, B. K. (1996). *Scales of Independent Behavior-Revised (SIB-R).* Rolling Meadows, IL: Riverside Publishing.

Burns, M. K., & Gibbons, K. (2008). *Response to intervention implementation in elementary and secondary schools: Procedures to assure scientific-based practices.* New York, NY: Routledge.

Campbell, A., & Anderson, C. M. (2008). Enhancing effects of check-in/check-out with function-based support. *Behavioral Disorders, 33,* 233–245.

Cartledge, G., & Kourea, L. (2008). Culturally responsive classrooms for culturally diverse students with and at risk for disabilities. *Exceptional Children, 74,* 351–371.

Castagno, A. E., & Brayboy, B. M. J. (2008). Culturally responsive schooling for indigenous youth: A review of the literature. *Review of Educational Research, 78,* 941–993.

Cavanagh, T. (2007). Focusing on relationships creates safety in schools. *Set: Research Information for Teachers, 1,* 31–35.

Centers for Disease Control and Prevention (2010). *Suicide: Facts at a glance.* Retrieved from http://www.cdc.gov/ViolencePrevention/pdf/Suicide_DataSheet-a.pdf

Cheney, D., Flower, A., & Templeton, T. (2008). Applying Response to Intervention metrics in the social domain for students at risk of developing emotional or behavioral disorders. *The Journal of Special Education, 42,* 108–126.

Cohen, J., McCabe, E. M., Michelli, N. M., & Pickeral, T. (2009). School climate: Research, policy, practice, and teacher education. *Teachers College Record, 111,* 180–213.

Community First Foundation (2009). Standard Response Protocol (SRP). Retrieved from http://givingfirst.org/index.cfm?fuseaction=Organizations.Programs&Organization

Cornell, D., & Sheras, P. (2006). *Guidelines for responding to student threats of violence.* Boston, MA: Sopris West Educational Services.

Curwin, R. L., & Mendler, A. N. (1999). *Discipline with dignity.* Alexandria, VA: Association for Supervision and Curriculum Development.

Daunic, A. P., Smith, S. W., Robinson, T. R., Miller, M. D., & Landry, K. L. (2000). Implementing schoolwide conflict resolution and peer mediation programs: Experiences in three middle schools. *Intervention in School & Clinic, 36(2),* 94–100.

Debski, J., Spadafore, C. D., Jacob, S., Poole, D. A., & Hixson, M. D. (2007). Suicide intervention: Training, roles, and knowledge of school psychologists. *Psychology in the Schools, 44,* 157–170.

Deno, E. (1970). Special education as developmental capital. *Exceptional Children, 37,* 229–237.

Dodge, K. A. (1980). Social cognition and children's aggressive behavior. *Child Development, 51,* 162–170.

Drewery, W. (2004). Conferencing in schools: Punishment, restorative justice, and the productive importance of the process of conversation. *Journal of Community & Applied Social Psychology, 14,* 332–344.

Dunlap, G., Sailor, W., Horner, R. H., & Sugai, G. (2009). Overview and history of positive behavior support. In W. Sailor, G. Dunlap, G. Sugai, & R. Horner (Eds.), *Handbook of Positive Behavior Support* (pp. 3–16). New York, NY: Springer.

Evans, I. M. (2010). Positive affective priming: A behavioral technique to facilitate therapeutic engagement by families, caregivers, and teachers. *Child & Family Behavior Therapy, 32,* 257–271.

Evans, I. M., Cicchelli, T., Cohen, M., & Shapiro, N. P. (1995). (Eds.). *Staying in school: Partnerships for educational change.* Baltimore, MD: Paul H. Brookes.

Evans, I. M., & Harvey, S. T. (2012). *Warming the emotional climate of the classroom: Understanding feelings in primary school.* Wellington, New Zealand: Dunmore Press.

Evans, I. M., & Meyer, L. H. (1985). *An educative approach to behavior problems: A practical decision model for interventions with severely handicapped learners.* Baltimore, MD: Paul H. Brookes Publishing.

Evans, I. M., Okifuji, A., Engler, L., Bromley, K., & Tishelman, A. (1993). Home-school communication in the treatment of childhood behavior problems. *Child & Family Behavior Therapy, 15,* 37–60.

Fein, R., Vossekuil, B., Pollack, W., Borum, R., Modzeleski, W., & Reddy, M. (2002). *Threat assessment in schools: an approach to prevent targeted violence* [NCJ 155000]. Washington, DC: National Institute of Justice. Retrieved from http://www.secretservice.gov/ntac/ntac_threat.pdf

Fergusson, D. M., Beautrais, A. L., & Horwood, L. J. (2003). Vulnerability and resiliency to suicidal behaviours in young people. *Psychological Medicine, 33,* 61–73.

Fuchs, D., Fuchs, L. S., & Stecker, P. M. (2010). The "blurring" of special education in a new continuum of general education placements and services. *Exceptional Children, 76,* 301–323.

Garrard, W. M., & Lipsey, M. W. (2007). Conflict Resolution Education and antisocial behavior in U.S. schools: A meta-analysis. *Conflict Resolution Quarterly, 25,* 9–38.

Gay, G. (2010). *Culturally responsive teaching* (2nd ed.). New York, NY: Teachers College Press.

Glynn, T., Berryman, M., Bidois, P., & Atvars, K. (1997). *Bilingual behavioural checklists: Initiating a student, teacher and parent partnership in behaviour management* (Unpublished paper). Poutama Pounamu Education Research Centre, Tauranga, New Zealand.

Goodman, R. (1997). The Strengths and Difficulties Questionnaire: A research note. *Journal of Child Psychology and Psychiatry, 38,* 581–586.

Gonzalez, N., Moll, L. C., & Amanti, C. (2005). *Funds of knowledge: Theorizing practices in households, communities, and classrooms.* Mahwah, NJ: Lawrence Erlbaum.

Greene, R. W. (2008). *Lost at school: Why our kids with behavioral challenges are falling through the cracks and how we can help them.* New York, NY: Scribner.

Gresham, F. M. (2005). Response to intervention: An alternative means of identifying students as emotionally disturbed. *Education and Treatment of Children, 28,* 328–344.

Gresham, F. M., & Elliott, S. N. (1990). *Social Skills Rating System.* Circle Pines, MN: American Guidance Service.

Hamilton Fish Institute on School and Community Violence (2007). *Foundations of successful youth mentoring: A guidebook for program development.* Washington, DC: The George Washington University.

Harry, B. (2008). Collaboration with culturally and linguistically diverse families: Ideal versus reality. *Exceptional Children, 74,* 372–388.

Hynds, A., Sleeter, C., Hindle, R., Savage, C., Penetito, W., & Meyer, L. H. (2011). Te Kotahitanga: A case study of a repositioning approach to teacher professional development for culturally responsive pedagogies. *Asia-Pacific Journal of Teacher Education, 39,* 339–351.

Individuals with Disabilities Education Improvement Act, 20 U.S.C. § 1400 *et seq.* (2004). (reauthorization of the Individuals with Disabilities Education Act of 1990).

Kane, J., Lloyd, G., McCluskey, G., Riddell, S., Stead, J., & Weedon, E. (2007). *Restorative practices in three Scottish councils: Final report of the evaluation of the first two years of the pilot projects 2004–2006.* Edinburgh: Scottish Executive. Retrieved from www.scotland.gov.uk/Publications/2007/08/24093135

Kleinfeld, J. (1975). Effective teachers of Eskimo and Indian students. *School Review, 83*, 301–344.

Martella, R. C., Nelson, J. R., & Marchand-Martella, N. E. (2003). *Managing disruptive behavior in schools: A schoolwide, classroom, and individualized social learning approach.* Boston, MA: Pearson Educational.

Maxwell, G., & Carroll-Lind, J. (1997). *The impact of bullying on children* (Research report No. 6). Wellington, New Zealand: Office of the Children's Commissioner.

McCluskey, G., Lloyd, G., Kane, J., Riddell, S., Stead, J., & Weedon, E. (2008). Can restorative practices in schools make a difference? *Educational Review, 60*, 405–417.

McIntosh, K., Campbell, A. L., Carter, D. R., & Zumbo, B. D. (2009). Concurrent validity of Office Discipline Referrals and cut points used in Schoolwide Positive Behavior Support. *Behavioral Disorders, 34*, 100–113.

Meyer, L. H., & Evans, I. M. (1989). *Nonaversive intervention for behavior problems: A manual for home and community.* Baltimore, MD: Paul H. Brookes.

Meyer, L. H., & Janney, R. E. (1989). User-friendly measures of meaningful outcomes: Evaluating behavioral interventions. *Journal of The Association for Persons with Severe Handicaps, 14*, 263–270. [Reprinted in Bambara, L. M., Dunlap, G., & Schwartz, I. S. (Eds.). (2004). Positive behavior support: Critical articles on improving practice for individuals with severe disabilities. Austin, TX: Pro-Ed.]

Ministry of Education Special Programs Branch. (1999). *Focus on suspension: A resource for schools.* Victoria, BC, Canada: British Columbia Crown Publications.

Mytton, J., DiGuiseppi, C., Gough, D., Taylor, R., & Logan S. (2006, July 19). School-based secondary prevention programmes for preventing violence. *Cochrane Database Systematic Reviews, 3*, Art. No. CD004606.

Nickerson, A. B., & Zhe, E. J. (2004). Crisis prevention and intervention: A survey of school psychologists. *Psychology in the Schools, 41*, 777–788.

Olweus, D. (1993). *Bullying at school: What we know and what we can do.* Oxford, UK: Blackwell.

Olweus, D. (2001). Peer harassment: A critical analysis and some important issues. In J. Juvonen & S. Graham (Eds.), *Peer harassment in school: The plight of the vulnerable and victimized* (pp. 3–20). New York, NY: Guilford Press.

Olweus, D. (2003). A profile of bullying at school. *Educational Leadership, 60(6)*, 12–17.

Ploeg, J., Ciliska, D., Dobbins, M., Hayward, S., Thomas, H., & Underwood, J. (1996). A systematic overview of adolescent suicide prevention programs. *Canadian Journal of Public Health, 87*, 319–324.

Poland, S., & Chartrand, D. (2008, April). Suicide prevention and schools. *District Administration, 44(5)*, 56–57.

Poland, S., & McCormick, J. S. (1999). *Coping with crisis: Lessons learned.* Longmont, CO: Sopris West.

Portzky, G., & van Heeringen, K. (2006). Suicide prevention in adolescents: A controlled study of the effectiveness of a school-based psycho-educational program. *Journal of Child Psychology and Psychiatry, 47*, 910–918.

President's Commission on Excellence in Special Education. (2002). *A new era: Revitalizing special education for children and their families.* Retrieved from http://ies.ed.gov/ncser/pdf/NLTS2_Discipline_FS_03_21_06.pdf

Prothrow-Stith, D. (1987). *Violence prevention curriculum for adolescents.* Newton, MA: Education Development Center.

Restorative Practices Development Team. (2003). *Restorative practices for schools: A resource.* Hamilton, New Zealand: University of Waikato School of Education.

Robinson, T. R., Smith, S. W., & Daunic, A. P. (2000). Middle school students' views on the social validity of peer mediation. *Middle School Journal, 31*(5), 23–29.

Rosen, L. (2005). *School discipline: Best practices for administrators* (2nd ed.). Thousand Oaks, CA: Corwin.

Ross, D. D., Bondy, E., Gallingane, C., & Hambacher, E. (2008). Promoting academic engagement through insistence: Being a warm demander. *Childhood Education, 84*, 142–146.

Savage, C. (2009). Culturally responsive behavior management. In V. Green & S. Cherrington (Eds.), *Delving into diversity: An international exploration of diversity in education* (pp. 35–44). New York, NY: Nova.

Savage, C., Hindle, R., Meyer, L. H., Hynds, A., Penetito, W., & Sleeter, C.E. (2011). Culturally responsive pedagogies in the classroom: Indigenous student experiences across the curriculum. *Asia-Pacific Journal of Teacher Education, 39*, 183–198.

Savage, C., Lewis, J., & Colless, N. (2011). Essentials for implementation: Six years of Schoolwide Positive Behaviour Support in New Zealand. *New Zealand Journal of Psychology, 40*, 29–37.

Schindler, H. R., & Horner, R. H. (2005). Generalized reduction of problem behavior of young children with autism: Building trans-situational interventions. *American Journal on Mental Retardation, 110*, 36–47.

Schwartz, D., Dodge, K. A., Pettit, G. S., & Bates, J. E. (1997). The early socialization of aggressive victims of bullying. *Child Development, 68*, 665–675.

Shields, C., Bishop, R., & Mazawi, A. (2005). *Pathologizing practices: The impact of deficit thinking on education.* New York, NY: Peter Lang.

Skiba, R. J., & Peterson, R. L. (1999). The dark side of zero tolerance: Can punishment lead to safe schools? *Phi Delta Kappan, 80*, 372–382.

Skiba, R. J., & Peterson, R. L. (2000). School discipline at a cross-roads: From zero tolerance to early response. *Exceptional Children, 66*, 335–347.

Skiba, R. J., Simmons, A. B., Ritter, S., Gibbs, A. C., Rausch, M. K., Cuadrado, J., & Chung, C.-G. (2008). Achieving equity in special education: History, status, and current challenges. *Exceptional Children, 74*, 264–288.

Sleeter, C. S. (2011). (Ed.). *Professional development for culturally responsive and relationship-based pedagogy.* New York, NY: Peter Lang.

Sleeter, C. E., & Grant, C. A. (2009). *Making choices for multicultural education: Five approaches to race, class, and gender* (6th ed.). Hoboken, NJ: Wiley.

Strong, K., & Cornell, D. (2008). Student threat assessment in Memphis City Schools: A descriptive report. *Behavioral Disorders, 34*, 42–54.

Sue, S. (1998). In search of cultural competence in psychotherapy and counseling. *American Psychologist, 53*, 440–448.

Sugai, G., Horner, R., Sailor, W., Dunlap, G., Eber, L., Lewis, T., et al. (2005). *Schoolwide Positive Behavior Support: Implementers' blueprint and self-assessment.* Washington, DC: Technical Assistance Center on Positive Behavioral Interventions and Supports.

Todd, A. W., Horner, R., & Dickey, C. R. (2010, August). SWIS Documentation Project Referral Form Examples, Version 4.4. Retrieved from http://www.swis.org/index.php?page=resources;rid=1025

Unnever, J. D., & Cornell, D. G. (2004). Middle school victims of bullying: Who reports being bullied? *Aggressive Behavior, 30*, 373–388.

Varnham, S. (2008). Keeping them connected: Restorative justice in schools in Australia and New Zealand—what progress? *Australia & New Zealand Journal of Law & Education, 13,* 71–82.

Valenzuela, A. (1999). *Subtractive schooling: U.S.-Mexican youth and the politics of caring.* Albany, NY: State University of New York Press.

Walker, H. M., Horner, R. H., Sugai, G., Bullis, M., Sprague, J. R., & Bricker, D., & Kaufman, M. J. (1996). Integrated approaches to preventing antisocial behavior patterns among school-age children and youth. *Journal of Emotional and Behavioral Disorders, 4,* 194–209.

Wanzek, J., & Vaughn, S. (2009). Students demonstrating persistent low response to reading intervention: Three case studies. *Learning Disabilities Research and Practice, 24,* 151–163.

Ware, F. (2006). Warm demander pedagogy: Culturally responsive teaching that supports a culture of achievement for African American students. *Urban Education, 41,* 427–456.

Wolfgang, C. H. (2005). *Solving discipline and classroom management problems: Methods and models for today's teachers* (6th ed.). Hoboken, NJ: Wiley.

Zehr, H. (1990). *Changing lenses.* Scottdale, PA: Herald Press.

Zehr, H. (2002). *The little book of restorative justice.* Intercourse, PA: Good Books.

Index

Page references followed by (table) indicate a table; followed by (figure) indicate an illustrated figure.

CORWIN
A SAGE Company

The Corwin logo—a raven striding across an open book—represents the union of courage and learning. Corwin is committed to improving education for all learners by publishing books and other professional development resources for those serving the field of PreK–12 education. By providing practical, hands-on materials, Corwin continues to carry out the promise of its motto: **"Helping Educators Do Their Work Better."**